Nice 'n Easy
■ Spanish ■
Grammar

Nice 'n Easy ■ Spanish ■ Grammar

SANDRA TRUSCOTT

McGraw-Hill

New York   Chicago   San Francisco   Lisbon   London   Madrid   Mexico City
Milan   New Delhi   San Juan   Seoul   Singapore   Sydney   Toronto

The McGraw·Hill Companies

Library of Congress Cataloging-in-Publication Data

Truscott, Sandra
     Nice 'n easy Spanish grammar / Sandra Truscott.
          p.   cm.
     Originally published: Pan Books, 1984.
     Includes index.
     ISBN 0-8442-9496-9
     1. Spanish language—Grammar—Handbooks, manuals, etc.

    PC4112 .T69   1998
    468.2'421—dc21   98-008724

14 15 16 17 18 19 20 21 22 23 24 25   VRS/VRS   0 9 8 7 6

ISBN-13: 978-0-8442-9496-4
ISBN-10:   0-8442-9496-9

McGraw-Hill books are available at special quantity discounts to use as premiums and sales promotions, or for use in corporate training programs. For more information, please write to the Director of Special Sales, Professional Publishing, McGraw-Hill, Two Penn Plaza, New York, NY 10121-2298. Or contact your local bookstore.

Also available

Nice 'n Easy French Grammar
Nice 'n Easy German Grammar

Sandra Truscott is an adult education teacher of Spanish. She is the co-author of the self-study course *Just Listen 'n Learn Spanish*.

Contents

Introduction

You may be going on a trip to Spain this year and may feel you ought to brush up on your Spanish. Or do you have an examination coming up which you are a bit nervous about? Or perhaps you've recently bought a phrase book but want to know how the language works so that you can break away from the standard formula. Whatever the reason, we hope this *Nice 'n Easy Grammar* will help you detect the structure behind the phrases that all travelers to Spain and Spanish-speaking countries come across sooner or later: **mañana**, **buenos días**, **¿qué tal?**

The key word here is 'help'. To help those who've 'missed out' on grammar, we've included a glossary of grammatical terms – the shorthand which language teachers use to describe words, what they do and how they behave in a sentence. We hope this book will not only be helpful, but also interesting. That's why we've made it as relevant as possible by taking examples from magazines, newspapers and the signs that you'll see all around you when you arrive in Spain. We've also tried to compare Spanish usage with the way the English language works – you might find that by the end of the book, you've learned some English grammar too!

Now for some hints on how to use this book. First of all, don't try to study it straight through from cover to cover. The chances are that you won't get much beyond p.10! Why not skim through it to get an idea of what it contains? – then use it as a simple and concise reference book: for looking up a tense that's been bothering you, or perhaps for more information on a grammatical point that you haven't fully understood in the course that you've been taking.

The exercises which follow each grammar point have been numbered according to difficulty. You'll need a dictionary to do the more difficult exercises – but don't feel discouraged if you don't understand everything. If the exercise is based on an extract, try to get the gist of it and remember that we are aiming to encourage you to think about the grammar point in question rather than the passage as a whole. Alternatively, you might like to skip the more difficult exercises until you feel more confident about using the language.

Above all, don't be put off by grammar. You don't have to know or remember it all to understand and be understood in Spanish. In fact, the more you refer to it the better, since you'll become more familiar, more readily, with the nuts and bolts of the language.

So good luck with your *Nice 'n Easy Grammar* – or as the Spanish say **'suerte'**!

NB: If you are traveling in South America, you won't notice many differences between grammatical usage there and in Spain. Latin Americans have simplified the dual system of direct and indirect objects (**le/lo/la** – see p.83) and telescoped them into one: and Argentinians use the old Spanish form **vos** instead of **tú**, with a special verb ending to accompany it. Otherwise, the major difference you will find between New and Old World Spanish is in vocabulary and pronunciation – which go beyond the scope of this book.

Glossary of grammar

Verbs

A verb is a word (or words) which expresses an action or describes a state:

Kathy *goes* to Spain next year
I *like* bullfights
Dad *is listening* to his cassette
the sea around here *is* very rough

When language teachers talk about verbs, they use other technical terms to describe them (see below).

INFINITIVE
This is the form of the verb used when talking about the action in general: it's the form that you will find in the dictionary when you look up the verb in question. There are three types of infinitives in Spanish with three different endings **-ar**, **-er** and **-ir**: English has only the one form, preceded by the word 'to':

mirar	to look
entender	to understand
pedir	to ask for or order

Infinitives never change their form, even when other verbs in the sentence do:

I like *to swim*
she likes *to swim*

ENDINGS
Once you've skimmed through this section on verbs, you will realize that the form of the verb changes very frequently. The basic part of the word (the *root* or *stem*) remains the same and the endings vary:

root	*ending*		
termin	**aba**	I was finishing	(**terminar** to finish)
mir	**ó**	he looked	(**mirar** to look)
cant	**amos**	we are singing	(**cantar** to sing)

Verb endings vary for three reasons – tense, person and mood.

TENSE

When we talk about tenses, we are dealing with time – happenings in the past, the present and the future. There are lots of different tenses in Spanish but they divide roughly into three: past tenses (e.g. the preterite), present tenses (e.g. the present continuous) and future tenses (e.g. the conditional).

PERSONS

These are the people responsible for the action:

I was watching TV last night
Mary came home late
we spent last year in Mexico

Spanish has more 'persons' than English: we have only one word for 'you' and one for 'they': Spanish has four forms for 'you' and two for 'they'.

The verb in Spanish is usually conjugated in the following way:

singular		*plural*	
I	1st person	we	1st person
you	2nd person	you	2nd person
he, she, it	3rd person	they	(two forms – one for women only, the other for men only or men and women)
you (**usted**)	3rd person	you (**ustedes**)	3rd person

Persons in the left hand column are called 'singular': they refer to only one person. Persons in the right hand column are called 'plural': they refer to more than one person. So language teachers or grammar books discussing the first person plural would be talking about 'we' (see, watch, look). First person singular would refer to the form 'I' (see, watch, look).

MOODS

Like English, Spanish has three 'moods' – the indicative, the subjunctive and the imperative. You probably won't be aware of these when you speak English, because we don't have the same variety of verb endings as in Spanish. Nevertheless, they do exist. Very generally speaking, the indicative mood deals with actions, events or facts which are positive and definite. The subjunctive deals with the dubious and uncertain, with wishes and possibilities. And the imperative is a command – telling people to do things, for instance, 'put that away!', 'clean your shoes!'.

REGULAR VERBS
When we talk about regular verbs, we mean verbs which follow a set pattern of endings. Once you have learned the endings for a regular **-ar** verb, for example, you can form unlimited numbers of this kind of verb, provided they are regular.

IRREGULAR VERBS
But not all verbs are regular! Irregular verbs are the odd ones out, verbs which change their form in the root or in the ending. As you familiarize yourself with Spanish, you will come to detect certain patterns between sets of irregular verbs – but unfortunately, many of these verbs simply have to be learned by heart. Irregular verbs tend to be the more commonly used ones – like **ir** (to go), **volver** (to return), **ser** (to be) – so it's well worth the effort of coming to grips with them at an early stage.

RADICAL-CHANGING VERBS
This is a class of verbs in between regular and irregular verbs. They are so called because they change their form in the root. The vowel **o** for instance, changes to **ue** in this sort of verb, so that **volver** (to return) becomes **vuelvo** (I return). Once you know that a verb is radical-changing, however, you can be sure that it will only change according to its prescribed pattern.

COMPOUND VERBS
These are verbs made up of two or more verbs, for example, 'I have been waiting', 'he had been singing'. The first verb (in these cases, 'have' and 'had') is called the auxiliary verb because it helps in the formation of the verb as a whole. The second part of the verb (here, 'waiting', 'singing') is known as the participle.

PARTICIPLE
This form of the verb is usually used along with the auxiliary. There are two forms – the present participle, which in English has the ending '-ing', e.g. 'looking', 'talking', 'reading' and the past participle, which in English often has the ending '-ed', e.g. 'looked', 'talked' etc. There are, however, exceptions to the rule. The past participle of 'to read' is 'read' – spelled the same as the infinitive but pronounced differently: in other words, 'to read' is an English irregular verb.

REFLEXIVE VERBS
These are verbs which refer back to the person doing the action (that is, to the subject – see p.41):

I *see myself* in the mirror
he *shaves himself* each morning

This sort of verb is quite common in Spanish – more so than in English. And it's sometimes difficult to see that the verb does indeed refer back to the person involved. We simply have to accept that in Spanish some verbs are reflexive and others are not. In any case, you will recognize them in the dictionary by the ending **se** ('himself', 'herself', 'oneself') tacked on to the end of the verb: **'levantarse'** to get (oneself) up.

IMPERSONAL VERBS

These are verbs which don't have a 'person' properly speaking – or where you can think of the person as 'one'. They are very common in Spanish, especially in signs and notices:

se prohibe fumar   one is forbidden to smoke/no smoking
aquí se habla francés   French spoken here

DIRECT AND REPORTED SPEECH

Direct speech is what we call a direct quotation of someone's actual words. The sentence will have quotation marks around it and a phrase like 'he said', 'I exclaimed', 'she shouted' will either precede or follow it:

'I'll come and see you tomorrow' he said

Reported speech is when we are informing someone of what a third person has said – but in an indirect way. There are no quotation marks and the two parts of the sentence are frequently linked with the word 'that':

he said that he would come and see me tomorrow

POSITIVE AND NEGATIVE SENTENCES

Positive sentences, commands or words tell us something definite – how something is, or what will happen:

it is an informative newspaper

A negative sentence tells us what someone or something is not – what has not or will not happen. It contains a word like 'no', 'not', 'nowhere', 'nobody' etc:

there's no one around at this time

ADVERBS

These are words which tell us more about verbs. They are easy to recognize in English by the ending '-ly': 'he walked slowly', 'she laughed loudly'. In Spanish adverbs often end in **-mente** : **lentamente**, slowly, **rápidamente**, quickly, **francamente**, frankly.

Nouns and adjectives

A noun is the label or name that we attach to a place, thing, person or idea. In English, the words 'a' or 'the' often precede them: a house, the table, a garden, freedom, happiness. Names of people (John Smith, Mary Jones) and of places (London, Paris. Madrid) are called proper nouns.

PRONOUNS
These are short words which replace nouns: we use them to avoid repetition and for the sake of brevity. Instead of repeating John Smith's name every time we refer to him, we say 'he'. 'He', 'she', 'it' etc. – these are all subject pronouns. Relative pronouns ('that', 'which', 'whom') link two parts of a sentence together:

there's the dog *that* I saw

In Spanish, reflexive pronouns are used a great deal (**me**, **te**, **se** etc.). These are the equivalents of 'myself', 'yourself', 'oneself' etc. in English.

GENDER
In English we often refer to ships or planes as 'she' although they are no more feminine than a table or a set of chairs. In Spanish, all nouns are either masculine or feminine in gender: table is feminine (**la mesa**), plane is masculine (**el avión**). There is no logic behind this: you can't tell by looking at the object if it fits into the masculine or feminine category (although the word endings will help you find out). It's useful to learn the gender of a noun along with each new word by remembering the article (p.54) that accompanies it.

NEUTER
You can, however, have an adjective or pronoun which is neuter. In Spanish a neuter form usually refers to a general idea:

lo bueno   the good
lo malo   the bad

ARTICLE
The definite article in English is 'the'. Spanish, however, has four different words for our one. These correspond to the masculine and feminine forms and to number (singular or plural). The articles in Spanish are **el**, **la**, **los**, and **las**.

INDEFINITE ARTICLE

'A' or 'an' in English, depending on whether the word begins with a consonant ('a mouse') or a vowel ('an orange'). Spanish also has two forms. **Un** is used with a masculine word and **una** with a feminine word: **un hombre**, **una naranja**.

SUBJECT

Nouns can be the subject or object of a sentence. The subject is the person or thing that performs the action:

Mary kicked the ball to Tom

OBJECT

In the sentence above, 'ball' is the direct object – it's on the receiving end of the action (in this case, at the end of Mary's foot!). The indirect object is Tom – also involved but not as directly as Mary or the ball. English indirect objects usually have the words 'to' or 'for' in front of them.

ADJECTIVES

These words tell you more about a noun or pronoun. They describe them in terms of color, shape, temperature, size etc:

an *elegant* country house
it was *large*, *fluffy* and *warm*

COMPARATIVES AND SUPERLATIVES

We can compare two nouns by using special forms of the adjective: in English we use the word 'more':

she was even more beautiful than her sister

or we can add '-er' to the end of the adjective:

he was quieter than his brother

Grammatically, this is called the comparative.

We can also compare more than two things in English by using the word 'most' or by adding the ending '-est' to the adjective:

it was the most amazing thing I'd ever seen
she was the loveliest bride of the year

This is called the superlative.

POSSESSIVE ADJECTIVES

In English these are words like 'my', 'your', 'his':

my raincoat and *his* umbrella

DEMONSTRATIVE ADJECTIVES

These are words like 'this', that', 'these', 'those':

this bus and *that* car

NOUNS

As you have seen, all Spanish nouns are either masculine or feminine: in general, a word ending in **-o** is masculine (**el niño**, the boy) and a word ending in **-a** is feminine (**la niña**, the girl). Some other endings **-ción**, (**la nación**, the nation), **-tad** (**libertad**, liberty), **-dad** (**la ciudad**, the city) tend to be feminine also. Other than these general guidelines, you must learn the gender of the noun along with its meaning.

PREPOSITIONS

These are short linking words which show the relationship between one word and another: 'at', 'in', 'on', 'to'. You'll be glad to know that they don't usually change their form.

IDIOMS

Are short, untranslatable phrases like **¿qué tal?** If you were to translate this literally it would make no sense at all; idioms must be learned and remembered all of a piece. It's important to remember here that language can rarely be translated word for word: there are few direct equivalents between one language and another. But then that's what makes languages so interesting! – and why learning phrases and words in context (that is, in a whole sentence or dialogue) is so helpful. Don't worry too much about idioms though – you can get by with knowing about a dozen of the more common ones. (And by the way, **¿qué tal?** means 'how are things?')

ACCENTS

The final item in our glossary are those marks which many languages use in their spelling to show changes in stress, meaning or pronunciation. You won't have to bother too much about this side of things if you are only interested in making yourself understood in spoken Spanish. But you'll soon notice the upside down question marks and exclamation marks in written Spanish – and the ˜ above the 'n' which changes the pronunciation from a simple 'n' to 'ny'.

All about grammar

Verbs

Some hints for dealing with verbs

Don't be depressed by the verb list on p.113 – there are ways of making things easier for yourself! First of all, don't try to learn too many verbs at one time. One verb a day is quite sufficient. (Having a daily target is a good idea – grammar does not always penetrate by osmosis!) Rather than learning verb tables with all the different persons, it's more useful to put the different forms in context. Find sentences in your Spanish phrase book that contain the verb you're studying: invent sentences for yourself and practice these. If you are taking a course, look out for examples which use the verb itself or a similar one. The thing is to use the verb in ordinary speech and not to isolate it as part of a table.

If you do find it all rather daunting, decide on learning only those tenses or parts of the verb which you are likely to use. You could get away with only learning one past tense (the preterite), the present tense and one form of the future, **voy a** . . . . Once you've got the hang of these, you can be more adventurous and try your hand with tenses which will give you more flexibility. And you don't need all four versions of 'you'. If you stick to **usted** or **ustedes**, you have the advantage of only having to learn four persons, instead of six: (remember that **usted** shares the same form as **él** and **ella**). Again once you've gained some confidence and want to make friends in Spain, then you can try using the **tú** and **vosotros** forms.

You will probably find that once you have come to grips with the basic four persons, the other forms will fall easily into place. Try to find some mnemonic or similarity of spelling which will help you remember the forms. In the present tense, the first person singular ends in **-o** – so, coincidentally, does the word for I, which accompanies it **yo**: **yo hablo**. In the third person, the ending is often **-e** and the **él** and **ella** which accompany it, begin with **e**: **él tiene** (he has) and **ella sabe** (she knows).

Remember to pick up the verb used by the person who is speaking to you. If he uses **hablar** in a question like **¿habla español?** then use **hablar** in your reply. Lots of people make things difficult for themselves by trying to dig out language they've learned in the past and not using the cues given to them by the native speaker. But also remember that you will probably have to change the form of the verb: when the person speaking to you says **¿habla español?** you reply **hablo español**. Otherwise, the sentence remains exactly the same.

Finally, if you decide to learn anything well, learn the verbs! They are important in Spanish because the endings give you so much information – about who is talking and when actions are taking place. Spanish does not need the subject pronouns (I, you, he etc.), so the clues as to who is doing the action are contained in the verb. Although you can say **yo hablo** (I speak), much more frequent is the form **hablo** (I speak). You can probably get away with using **yo** to make it clear that you're talking about yourself – but the native speaker will not necessarily be similarly obliging. So do try to get these forms sorted out.

The present tense

IN ENGLISH: The present tense is used to denote action now – what is happening at the moment or what happens regularly. There are three ways of expressing the present in English:

I do speak English (sometimes)   I am speaking Spanish (at this moment)
I speak French (regularly, in France)

IN SPANISH: These three forms can be translated by one word:

hablo	I do speak	**vivo**	I do live
	I am speaking		I am living
	I speak		I live

Don't try to translate the words 'do' or 'am' – stick to the main verb.

WHEN TO USE
As we said in the glossary, there are only approximate equivalents between languages – that is, they only overlap to a point. So Spanish uses its present tense to convey ideas that we convey differently in English – e.g. by using another tense:

* when discussing something about to happen:
  vamos a la playa por la tarde   we'll be going to the beach this afternoon

- when using the verb **hacer** to do/make meaning 'ago':

  le vi hace dos minutos   I saw him two minutes ago

- and when using the phrase **desde hace** to mean for or since:

  estudio español desde hace un   I've been learning Spanish for a
  año   year

You'll see here that both **estudio** and **hace** are in the present tense. It's **estudio** because although you began studying Spanish a year ago, you're still studying it now.

1. Forming the present tense

There are three different sorts of verbs in Spanish – verbs which end in **-ar**, **-er** and **-ir**.

Comprar (to buy) is a good example of an **-ar** verb:

yo compro	I buy	**nosotros compramos**	we buy
tú compras	you buy	**vosotros compráis**	you buy
él compra	he buys	**ellos compran**	they buy
ella compra	she buys	**ellas compran**	they buy (women)
usted compra	you buy	**ustedes compran**	you buy

You don't need to use the word for 'I', 'you', 'he' and so on: most of the verb endings are different, so it's obvious *who* is performing the action.

Comer (to eat) is a typical **-er** verb:

yo como	**nosotros comemos**
tú comes	**vosotros coméis**
él come	**ellos comen**
ella come	**ellas comen**
usted come	**ustedes comen**

Vivir (to live) is a typical **-ir** verb:

	vivo		**vivimos**
	vives		**vivís**
él		**ellos**	
ella }	**vive**	**ellas** }	**viven**
usted		**ustedes**	

2. Irregular verbs

Unfortunately, there are a number of verbs which are irregular in their formation. These also happen to be the most common verbs, like **tener** (to have), **ir** (to go) and **ser** (to be). You will find a verb list on p.113. There are a number of other verbs which are irregular principally in the first person of the present tense, like **conocer** to know (**conozco** I know), **estar** to be (**estoy** I am). These also appear in the section on verbs on p.118 and 119.

3. Radical-changing verbs
These verbs have the same endings as the normal present tense but they change their roots.

● **o** to **ue**: verbs with an **o** in the root change this to **ue**. A typical example is **contar** (to tell or count):

cuento	contamos
cuentas	contáis
cuenta	cuentan

● **e** to **ie**: verbs that have **e** in the stem change this to **ie**. **Pensar** (to think) is a common example:

pienso	pensamos
piensas	pensáis
piensa	piensan

● **e** to **i**: finally verbs which end in -**ir** and have **e** in the stem change this to -**i**. e.g. **pedir** (to ask/order):

pido	pedimos
pides	pedís
pide	piden

Note that radical changing verbs have regular endings, and that no change takes place in the first and second person plural.

It's also worth remembering that some very common verbs are radical changing – verbs like **cerrar** to close (**cierro** I close), **empezar** to begin (**empiezo** I begin), **sentarse** to sit down (**me siento** I sit down).

HANDY PHRASES
You will find that you will soon learn this tense since it's easily the most common. The following phrases all have a verb in the present tense – and they're all phrases you might use or hear on your first day in Spain.

es caro/barato	it's expensive/cheap
soy americano/americana	I'm American
¿qué desea?	what would you like?
¿cómo está?	how are you?
no importa	it doesn't matter
¿cómo dice?	what did you say?
viajo solo	I'm traveling alone

PRACTICE

And now to help you practice your newly acquired skills, here are a few exercises for you to complete. The answers can be found in the section beginning on p.101.

1 Try conjugating (giving the full forms of) the two verbs below:

vender   to sell   **mirar**   to look

2 Here are two columns of statements. The first says where you are from (**soy de ...**), the second where you live (**vivo en ...**). Match up the statements which make the most sense.

soy de Italia   vivo en Edimburgo
soy de Francia   vivo en Londres
soy de Alemania   vivo en Milán
soy de los Estados Unidos   vivo en Hamburgo
soy de Escocia   vivo en Nueva York
soy de Inglaterra   vivo en París

3 You're in a souvenir shop. Which of the following remarks would you be most likely to make?

es muy caro
sólo bebo agua
está en el segundo piso

You're at the reception desk of your hotel. Would you hear?

aquí está su pasaporte, señor
¡oiga, camarero!
quiero una cerveza

You're on the terrace of a café. Would you say?

me duele la cabeza
dos cafés por favor
soy de Nueva York

4 Finally, here's the plot of a film made in English but dubbed into Spanish. Unfortunately, the story got rather complicated. Can you unravel it and put each sentence into the correct order?

A partir de ahí, los hechos se complican.
La historia se sitúa en los años treinta.
Alarmados, van al lugar.
¿Porqué no le preguntan a Evans? son sus palabras.

Se inicia cuando el joven John y el médico del pueblo oyen un grito. Al fondo de un acantilado, ven a un hombre herido.

Before you check your answers, here's something to think about:

el dinero no trae la felicidad pero cuando se va, se la lleva . . . .

The future tense

IN ENGLISH: The future tense is used for happenings that are yet to take place. We usually recognize it by the words 'will' or 'shall' before the main verb:

I'll go out soon
will you come with me?

Not strictly a future, but used to imply future, is the expression 'I'm going to . . .':

I'm going to iron my dress

IN SPANISH: We use the future in the same way:

te veré mañana	I'll see you tomorrow
¿vendrás a casa?	Will you come home?

As in the present tense, you only need one word to imply future where English needs two:

veré	I will see
¿vendrás?	will you come?

There is also an equivalent to the English 'going to' **voy a ...**

voy a ver a mi vecina   I'm going to call on my neighbor

When reducing the number of tenses you want to tackle, it might be just as well to concentrate on this particular form, since it is easier for a beginner. More about this one later.

WHEN TO USE
●   Spanish also uses the future when probability is implied:

¿dónde está Tom en estos días?	where's Tom these days?
estará en España	he must be in Spain

• on the other hand, Spanish doesn't need the future in a sentence such as:

will you ask the waiter to bring a glass of water?

If you think about this one, the questioner is really asking her companion to speak to the waiter – now. So Spanish translates this by using the present tense of **querer**, or by a command:

¿quiere pedir un vaso de agua?
pida un vaso de agua al camarero

1. Forming the future
This tense is an easy one to form. Start with the infinitive of the verb and add the following endings:

ir	to go		
ir	é	ir	emos
ir	ás	ir	éis
ir	á	ir	án

The endings are the same for **-ar**, **-er** and **-ir** verbs, so it's not very complicated.

2. Irregular forms of the future
Some future forms, however, don't start with the infinitive, but have evolved a different stem. For example, the verb **decir** to say does not use the infinitive form as its stem, but shortens it to **dir....** The endings, however, are the same as for the regular future tenses:

diré	diremos
dirás	diréis
dirá	dirán

Other examples of irregular futures are **vendré** I will come (**venir**), **pondré** I will put (**poner**), **saldré** I will go out (**salir**). Look at the verb list on p.119 for more examples.

3. I'm going to/voy a ...
You may find it simpler to convey the idea of future action by using **voy a ...** I'm going to. It's always followed by the infinitive:

voy a broncearme al sol	**vamos a ......**
vas a	**vais a ......**
va a	**van a ......**

Strictly speaking, this kind of future is more immediate than the ordinary future tense – but this won't matter too much in ordinary conversation.

HANDY PHRASES

You might hear this tense in the doctor's office when he says:

le pondré una inyección	I'll give you an injection

or:

le daré un antibiótico	I'll give you an antibiotic

Alternatively, you might see something like this on a poster:

se celebrará corrida de toros el 12 de agosto	there will be a bullfight on the 12th of August

Or in a shoe store window you might see:

no podremos admitir nuevos arreglos hasta la semana que viene	we will be unable to accept further repairs until next week

The weather forecast in the local newspaper could read something like this:

continuarán cielos despejados y ambiente muy caluroso	clear skies and hot weather will continue

And your horoscope might say:

captará un mundo desconocido pero fascinante	you will be caught up in a new and fascinating world

Using the simple **voy a** form, the doctor might say:

voy a darle unas pastillas	I'm going to give you some tablets

or:

voy a ponerle a régimen	I'm going to put you on a diet

And at your hotel, a Spanish friend could ask you to go swimming with him:

voy a la piscina; ¿vas a venir conmigo?	I'm going to the pool; are you going to come with me?

or:

voy a la discoteca esta tarde. ¿Quieres acompañarme?	I'm going to go to the disco tonight. Do you want to come with me?

PRACTICE

1 You're going to Spain next week. Using the verbs below, tell your neighbor what you plan to do. You can either use the **voy a ...** form or the straight future:

ir	estar	viajar	comer	beber
visitar	bailar	nadar	mirar	escuchar

2 Now for a piece about a band that's just about to burst onto the Spanish pop scene. Underline the verbs in the future and then give their infinitive forms:

La semana que viene, grabarán su primer disco, un single que saldrá al mercado a finales de mayo, editado por Estrella Cuatro: se anunciará una espectacular presentación del grupo en Madrid. Ya han empezado a lloverles los contratos de galas veraniegas ... Usted querrá saber más de ellos.

3 Here's a job advertisement for a sales manager for which you would like to apply. There are lots of verbs in the future. Use these to tell your wife (or husband) what you're going to have to do and know – if you get the job!

Gran Empresa Necesita

JEFE DE VENTAS

(Ref. 11. 843 C)

Será responsable de la promoción y ventas en su zona. Deberá poseer buena capacidad de organización y tener un conocimiento del mercado de hostería. Tendrá que vivir en Barcelona. Será preciso hablar catalán. Deberá aportar una gran capacidad para las relaciones sociales.

Escribir a

PELA Ref. N.2 571 E Gran Via 100, Madrid 14

---

a) ...... de la promoción y ventas en mi zona.
b) ...... poseer buena capacidad de organización.
c) ...... vivir en Barcelona.
d) ...... preciso hablar catalán.
e) ...... aportar una gran capacidad para las relaciones sociales.

NB: The answers to all these exercises can be found on p.101.

The conditional tense

IN ENGLISH: The conditional tense is related to the future tense: it has been called the future in the past, because it often occurs after a past tense. For example, instead of 'he says he will see you soon' we have 'he said he would see you soon'. The conditional can be recognized by the words 'would' or 'should'.

The conditional is also used when you are making inquiries in a polite and formal way:

would you like a drink?

and in what we call conditional clauses:

if I were rich, I would fly on the Concorde.

IN SPANISH: The conditional is used in much the same way:

dijo que estaría de vuelta dentro de unos días	he said he would be back within a few days
quisiera beber algo	I'd like something to drink

(**quisiera** is not strictly conditional but it's always used in the polite phrase 'I would like'. In fact it's probably the most commonly used 'conditional').

si tuviera dinero, iría al Perú   if I had the money, I'd go to Peru.

However, where 'should' indicates obligation – you ought to do something – don't use the conditional: use the present tense of **deber** to have to:

debes acostarte ahora   you should go to bed now

1. Forming the conditional
As with the future tense, start off with the infinitive and then add the following endings:

tomar	to take		
tomar	**ía**	**tomar**	**íamos**
tomar	**ías**	**tomar**	**íais**
tomar	**ía**	**tomar**	**ían**

This applies to all three verb endings.

2. Forming irregular conditionals

Verbs which have irregular stems in the future retain these in the conditional. The endings however always remain the same:

diría I would say
tendría I would have

HANDY PHRASES

You're in a taxi and you want to know how much the ride to Cullera might cost:

¿cuánto costaría un viaje a Cullera?

You're in your hotel and you need more hangers and blankets:

quisiera más perchas por favor
quisiera más mantas por favor

You're at a travel agency and you need to change your reservation:

quisiera cambiar mi reserva para el 8 de septiembre

or you need to cancel it completely:

quisiera anular mi reserva para el 16 de febrero

PRACTICE

1 Using the conditional, tell us what you would do if you won the lottery:

si ganara a la lotería comprar un helicóptero
viajar a Méjico
beber sólo champán
comer todos los días en el Ritz
escribir mi autobiografía

2 Here are two opinion polls, the first on Spain's entry into NATO (**OTAN**), the second on anti-terrorism and cooperation with the police. Choose and then circle your reply.

Si mañana se celebrase un referéndum
a) votaría a favor del ingreso en la OTAN
b) votaría en contra
c) me abstendría
d) no contestaría

Si llamaran a su puerta para registrar la casa
a) aceptaría sin sentirme molesto

b) aceptaría pero me sentiría molesto
c) no aceptaría sin mandamiento judicial

3 The last exercise is based on a rather disturbing piece about what might happen in the event of a nuclear war. We've omitted all the verbs in the conditional tense and put them in a list at the bottom of the extract. Can you put them back where they belong?

El gobierno prevé muchas infecciones dentro de los refugios que ...... ser tratadas con medecina casera. Pero los médicos estiman que los supervivientes ...... al salir otras infecciones que no .... fácilmente. No ...... posibilidad de inmunizar a los niños, que ...... muchas posibilidades de contraer difterias y poliomielitis.
Los supervivientes ...... graves riesgos de contraer infecciones bacteriales. La bacteria 'clásica' ...... epidemias de fiebres tifoideas y de cólera.

podrían	habría	provocaría	se solucionarían
tendrían	correrían	encontrarían	

The imperfect tense

IN ENGLISH: The imperfect tense is used for an action in the past which was continuous but not completed:

I was riding my bike this morning, when ... .

IN SPANISH: The imperfect tense is also used, as in English, to translate what was happening when something else occurred:

iba de tiendas cuando encontré a   I was out shopping when I met
   Felipe   Felipe

The first of these verbs is in the imperfect ('I was ...ing') and the second is a preterite (see p.30).

Use the imperfect for repeated or habitual action – where English uses the phrase 'I used to':

me bañaba todos los días   I used to go swimming every day

WHEN TO USE

- use the imperfect when you're describing things in the past:

   el sol brillaba y hacía viento   the sun shone and the wind blew

- and in general for events in the past that don't have a definite beginning or end:

   Eleanor se ponía cada vez más   Eleanor became more and more
   triste   upset

1. Forming the imperfect
In Spanish there are two sets of verb endings for the imperfect – one for **-ar** verbs, the other for **-er** and **-ir** verbs. These endings are added to the stem:

cantar	to sing	aprender	to learn
cantaba	cantábamos	aprendía	aprendíamos
cantabas	cantabais	aprendías	aprendíais
cantaba	cantaban	aprendía	aprendían

2. Three irregular imperfects
You'll be relieved to know that there are only three verbs which are irregular in the imperfect (see below):

Ir	to go	ver	to see	ser	to be
iba	íbamos	veía	veíamos	era	éramos
ibas	ibais	veías	veíais	eras	erais
iba	iban	veía	veían	era	eran

HANDY PHRASES
When describing what your vacation resort was like, you will want to use the word **hay** (there is/are) in the imperfect:

había un banco en la esquina   there was a bank on the corner
había una peluquería enfrente   there was a hairdresser's shop
                                    across the street

If you had to go to the dentist while in Spain, you might describe your symptoms later in the following terms:

me dolían las muelas   I had a toothache
necesitaba pastillas   I needed tablets

Or if you had to visit the doctor:

tenía fiebre   I had a high temperature
tenía gripe   I had the flu

You might want to describe your campsite:

era un camping autorizado   it was an official campsite
había duchas muy propias   there were very clean showers
íbamos todos los días a la playa – we used to go to the beach every
    era de arena   day – it was a sandy beach

PRACTICE
Now, why not try these exercises to make sure you've really assimilated the imperfect tense?

1 First of all, read this account of a love affair. We'll bring you back to earth by asking you to underline all the verbs in the imperfect tense – remember to concentrate on the gist of the passage and the verbs. Don't worry if you don't understand every word.

   Estaba un verano en París y conocí a una chica francesa – me enamoré de ella. Vivía en Estados Unidos, así que me fui a Nueva York con un billete de ida y vuelta y doscientos dólares. Llegué peor que un emigrante – los emigrantes solían tener contrato de trabajo y yo no tenía. Pero a los seis meses, trabajaba en un banco y enviaba dinero todos los meses a mi novia en Francia.

   Some of the verbs in the above passage are in the preterite tense. Try to understand why the author uses the preterite in certain cases and the perfect in others. (If you need help with this, turn to p.30.)

2 Now imagine someone asks you what you were doing when ... ¿**qué hacía cuando ...** ? Reply using the following phrases. Then see if you can make up any sentences of your own.

   montar a bicicleta
   nadar en la piscina
   tomar un café
   hacer footing por el parque
   cambiar dinero en el banco
   comprar un vestido en Galerías Preciados
   ver escaparates

3 Finally, someone caught up in a bank robbery recounts her experiences. Now tell us how it feels to be a bank robber by putting the italicized verbs in the first person. You'll have to change **se** to **me**.

   Todo el rato *se disculpaba* por lo que *hacían*: *decían* que *estaban* en el paro y que *querían comprarse* un coche. *Tenían* mucho miedo porque *veían* a la policía fuera del banco. También *veían* las cámaras de televisión y el público ...

The preterite tense

IN ENGLISH: We use this tense for events in the past which are over and done with. In contrast with the imperfect (p.27) the preterite deals with definite time limits, either expressed or implied:

I sang with the choir last night
I went to the hairdresser's yesterday

IN SPANISH: The preterite is used probably more than any other past tense. If you want to skip the other past tenses – fine, but don't skip this one if you want to be able to talk about past events.

Students tend to get confused about when to use the imperfect and when to use the preterite – especially in phrases like 'we lived in San Francisco for four years'. Is this a description – or something final? The thing to remember is that Spanish uses the preterite for events in the past, even if they took place over a long period of time – as long as that period is over, so:

vivimos en San Francisco durante cuatro años

WHEN TO USE
● some verbs change their meaning slightly in the preterite:

conocer means to know (a person) but,
le conocí en Madrid   I first met him in Madrid
saber means to know (a fact) but,
lo supo inmediatamente   he found out immediately
querer means to want but,
quise hacerlo   I tried to do it
and **no quise hacerlo**   I refused to do it

1. Forming the preterite
There are two sets of endings, one for **-ar** verbs and the other for **-er/ir** verbs. These are attached directly to the stem:

comprar to buy			**aprender** to learn		
compr é		compr amos	aprend í		aprend imos
compr aste		compr asteis	aprend iste		aprend isteis
compr ó		compr aron	aprend ió		aprend ieron

2. Forming irregular preterites

Unfortunately, as with any other tense that's used a great deal, there are lots of irregular forms. We've divided these into four sections, beginning with the most irregular.

a) There are three verbs which don't really follow any set pattern – **dar** (to give), **ir** (to go) and **ser** (to be). The preterite of **dar** is:

di	dimos
diste	disteis
dio	dieron

Oddly enough, **ser** (to be) and **ir** (to go), two of the most common verbs, share a form for the preterite:

fui	fuimos
fuiste	fuisteis
fue	fueron

It's always clear, though, from the context, what the sentence means:

fui a Mallorca el año pasado	I went to Mallorca last year
mi padre fue editor de periódico	my father was a newspaper editor

Because of this dual meaning, **fui** is a crucial form – make sure you learn it!

b) Verbs which are irregular in the first person and whose forms derive directly from that. Once you know the first person singular you can follow the pattern through, according to the normal endings. Let's take **andar** (to walk) as an example. (You will find other common verbs of this sort in the verb list on p.116.)

anduve	anduvimos
anduviste	anduvisteis
anduvo	anduvieron

There are two things to note about these verbs:

● first, they have no accents – unlike normal preterite forms.

● secondly, they divide into loose groups according to endings. **Andar** (to walk), **estar** (to be) and **obtener** (to obtain) all have similar endings in **-uve**. Why not try grouping these irregular verbs into 'families'? You'll find it easier to memorize them if you can see an underlying pattern.

c) Do you remember the stem-changing verbs in the present tense? (If you don't, see p.19.) Those ending in **-ir** occur again here:

● in verbs with stems in **o**, **o** becomes **u** in the third person (sing. and pl.); e.g. **dormir** (to sleep):

durmió he slept   **durmieron** they slept

● in verbs with stems in **e**, **e** becomes **i** in the third person (sing. and pl.); e.g. **pedir** (to ask/order):

pidió he asked   **pidieron** they asked

d) Finally, irregularities in spelling. You can skip this section if you aren't going to write Spanish. Quite simply, in order to keep the same sound running all the way through the verb, the spelling of the first person singular has to change in certain verbs. Again, there are four instances in which this occurs.

● **z** changes to **c** before **e**, e.g. **cruzar** to cross in the first person:

crucé I crossed   but **cruzó** he/she/you crossed
empecé I began   but **empezó** he/she/you began

c changes to **qu** before **e**, e.g. **buscar** to look for **c** changes to **qué** in the first person:

busqué I looked for   but **buscó** he/she/you looked for
saqué I took out   but **sacó** he/she/you took out
toqué I touched   but **tocó** he/she/you touched

● **g** changes to **gu** before **e**, e.g. **jugar** to play the **g** acquires another **u** in the first person:

jugué I played   but **jugó** he/she/you played

● and finally, some verbs acquire an extra **y** in the third person (sing. and pl.):

caí I fell down   but **cayó**   he/she/you fell down
creí I believed   but **creyó**   he/she/you believed
leí I read   but **leyeron** they/you read

HANDY PHRASES

You're talking about your travel arrangements. A Spanish friend might ask you:

¿hubo tren directo?	was there a direct train?
¿hubo que pagar algún suplemento?	did you have to pay an additional fare?
¿a qué hora llegaste?	what time did you arrive?

You're asking that same friend about a soccer game; you might say to him:

¿a qué hora empezó el partido?	what time did the game begin?
¿a qué hora terminó?	what time did it end?
¿cuánto te costaron las entradas?	how much did the tickets cost?
¿quién ganó?	who won?

Later, you describe what happened in the bank:

por la mañana, quise cambiar moneda americana	in the morning I tried to change American money
me dieron tres mil quinientas pesetas	they gave me 3,500 pesetas
hubo una cola muy larga	there was a very long line

That **hubo** is quite useful – it's the preterite equivalent of:

hay there is/there are (present)
había there was/there were (imperfect)

PRACTICE

1 Here are some extracts from the obituary column of a Spanish newspaper. Can you understand what they mean?

a) Nació en Londres, falleció en Nueva York a los sesenta y nueve años.

b) Murió en Panamá a los setenta y ocho años.

c) Falleció repentinamente en su casa de Madrid. Contaba cien años de edad.

2 Now match these pairs of phrases:

fui al banco	para broncearme al sol
visité España	para cambiarme de ropa
volví a mi habitación	pero no quedaban asientos
conocí a Juan	para cambiar dólares americanos
quise comprar una entrada	el año pasado en Gerona

3 Read this account of what happened to a man on a certain Tuesday night. Then change the person of the verb, so that you are the one telling the story. Remember, if the verb is reflexive you have to change **se** to **me**.

A las ocho y cuarto de la tarde del martes pasado, se lavó las manos y la cara, se cambió de ropa y salió de la casa. Fue al pueblo para reunirse con los amigos. Cruzó las vías. Caminó por encima de la vía y vio un tren al otro lado. Vio a dos chicos jóvenes debajo de las ruedas … pareció un poco raro pero no le dio mucha importancia.

4 Finally, here's the story of how a company built a house – only the verbs aren't in the preterite. Can you do this, using the **nosotros** form?

(Empezar) por el tejado: luego (bajar) hasta los cimientos. (Hacer) chimeneas, azulejos y pavimentos. (Pintar) y (barnizar) todo por dentro y por fuera. (Construir) persianas y macetas. Y (volver) al techo.

By the way, have you noticed that the regular **nosotros** form of the preterite is the same as the present tense?

The perfect tense

IN ENGLISH: The perfect tense is used for an event or action in the past which is somehow connected to the present: perhaps because it's a very recent happening or because, although begun in the past, it is still continuing.

The perfect is made up of two elements – the verb 'to have', and the past participle.

have you finished your homework? (this evening)
he's been teaching Spanish for two two years (and is still doing so)

IN SPANISH: The perfect tense is both used and formed in much the same way as in English with the verb 'to have' and the past participle. But instead of **tener**, Spanish uses the auxiliary verb **haber**, formed in the following way:

he	**hemos**
has	**habéis**
ha	**han**

The past participle has two endings, **-ado** for **-ar** verbs and **-ido** for **-er/ir** verbs:

ganado	earned	**he ganado**	I have earned
comido	eaten	**he comido**	I have eaten

It is helpful to think of the **-ado/ido** ending as equivalent to the '-ed' ending in English.

1. Irregular past participles
Of course, there are always some verbs that don't conform to the pattern we've described. However, the **haber** part of the verb remains unchanged – it's the past participle that varies.

he visto	I have seen
he hecho	I have done/made
he puesto	I have put

There is a complete list of these irregular past participles at the back of the book.

NB: Look at the English example given on p.34. Here the two parts of the verb were separated by the word 'you': 'have you finished?' In Spanish you must always keep the two parts of the perfect tense together, even if you have extra short words in the sentence like **me**, **usted** or **no**:

la familia se ha marchado	the family has gone away
¿no has cenado todavía?	haven't you had dinner yet?
¿ha querido usted venir?	did you want to come?

HANDY PHRASES
You've been having problems on vacation in Spain and have had to go to the police station. You might say:

hemos tenido un accidente	we've had an accident
he encontrado este bolso	I've found this purse
he perdido mi pasaporte	I've lost my passport

At the dentist, you may need the following phrases (though we hope not!):

se me ha caído un empaste	I've lost a filling
se me ha roto un diente	my tooth has broken

Going through customs you might need to say:

he llevado sólo cosas personales	I've only brought personal belongings
he abierto la maleta ya	I've already opened my bag

PRACTICE

1 The auxiliary has been omitted in these sentences. Can you complete each verb?

a) ¿España . . . cambiado mucho después de Franco?
b) Oye, ¿. . . visto ET?
c) ¿. . . telefoneado tu madre?
d) Mi esposo y yo ... visitado el Prado por la mañana.
e) ¿. . . venido tus padres?

2 Now for the same exercise the other way around. We'll give you the main verb in the infinitive form and you must change it into a past participle. You might have to look up the verb in the verb section on p.113, if you suspect it's irregular.

You're replying to the question **¿Qué han hecho hoy?**

a) Hemos (comer) en el nuevo restaurante en la Plaza de San Martín.
b) Hemos (tomar) café en el bar enfrente de la casa.
c) Hemos (ir) de compras.
d) Hemos (comprar) un nuevo traje para Juan y una chaqueta para Sonia.
e) Hemos (leer) El País y Cambio 16.

3 Here is an extract from an interview with a famous American film director. Study the questions and answers, both of which should contain examples of the perfect tense. However, these have been omitted from the passage and listed at the end of the exercise. Can you put them back in their correct positions?

a) En su última película, ... usted a un actor famoso.
pero el papel femenino .... dárselo a una desconocida.
¿Porqué?
b) Porque quería una personal absolutamente normal, inocente. La inocencia ... . muy necesaria.

c) ¿Su carrera … …… un camino diferente al que usted esperaba?
d) Sí, por lo de la televisión. Antes el único medio de entretenimiento era el cine. Pero ahora el medio …… y los jóvenes …… que adaptarse.
e) Sus películas no son entretenimiento ligero: ¿son algo más?
f) Si, siempre … …… evitar que aburran. Es una cuestión de gusto, nada más.
   Gracias.

ha sido   ha elegido   ha cambiado   ha preferido   han tenido   ha seguido   he intentado.

The pluperfect

IN ENGLISH: When you use the auxiliary verb 'had' and a past participle in sentences like:

I had visited my son last week
I had eaten my dinner when …

you are in fact using the pluperfect tense.

IN SPANISH: You use this tense just as you would in English, i.e. to translate verbs like 'had done' (**había hecho**), 'had seen' (**había visto**) and 'had gone home' (**había ido a casa**). It is of course related to the perfect: use the perfect for direct speech and the pluperfect for reported speech:

ha perdido el maletín (direct)   he's lost his briefcase
dijo que había perdido el maletín   he said he had lost his briefcase
   (reported)

1. Forming the pluperfect tense
Just like the perfect tense, the pluperfect tense has two parts: the auxiliary verb **haber** and the past participle. This time, though, you use the imperfect tense of **haber**:

había comprado	habíamos comprado
habías comprado	habíais comprado
había comprado	habían comprado

In all other respects, the pluperfect is just like the perfect tense.

2. Direct and reported speech

The more you study examples of Spanish usage, the more familiar you will become with the way the language works.

ha tenido que escribir una carta al abogado	he's had to write a letter to his lawyer
dijo que había tenido que escribir una carta al abogado	he said he'd had to write a letter to his lawyer
ha publicado un libro de poesía y una novela	he's published a poetry book and a novel
declaró que había publicado un libro de poesía y una novela	he stated that he had published a poetry book and a novel
ha visto la nueva película de Carlos Saura	he's seen the new film by Carlos Saura
mencionó que había visto la nueva película de Carlos Saura	he mentioned that he'd seen the new film by Carlos Saura
María no ha querido entrar en detalles	María has refused to go into too much detail
nos dijeron que María no había querido entrar en detalles	they told us that María had refused to go into too much detail
se ha mencionado una cifra de ochenta millones de pesetas	a sum of 80 million pesetas has been mentioned
los periódicos habían mencionado una cifra de ochenta millones de pesetas	the newspapers had mentioned a sum of 80 million pesetas

PRACTICE

1 Can you make these simple perfect verbs pluperfect? Remember the past participle stays the same:

he hecho; ha sido; hemos visto; han dicho; has querido.

2 The same sort of exercise – but this time in context. These sentences concern a mystery illness!

   a) Se han contado muchas historias sobre la enfermedad del presidente.

   b) En los últimos años han sido muchos los casos parecidos en España.

   c) Casi toda la población mayor de treinta años ha estado en contacto con el virus.

The progressive tenses

IN ENGLISH: We use progressive tenses a great deal. They are sometimes called continuous tenses and this clearly indicates what they are – verbs which stress the continuing nature of an action:

I am doing some sewing
I was looking at television

IN SPANISH: We have exactly the same sort of construction. Those of you who have studied French will remember that you cannot translate the progressive into French – so in this respect at least, Spanish is more like English than is French. But remember that **hablo** means I am speaking, as well as I speak, so don't use the progressive in Spanish unless you really mean that the action is going on right now.

1. Forming the progressive tenses
Spanish also uses two separate verbs to form the one construction – **estar** (to be), and the present participle which is formed in the following way:

● for **-ar** verbs add the ending **-ando** to the stem: **tomando** (taking)

● for **-er** and **-ir** verbs add **-iendo** to the stem: **comiendo** (eating), **viviendo** (living)

Place both parts of the verb together and you have a progressive present:

estoy comiendo (un bocadillo)   I'm eating (a sandwich)
está viendo (la televisión)   she's watching (television)

To form the progressive imperfect, use the imperfect tense of **estar** and the present participle:

estaba escuchando la radio   he was listening to the radio

You can make progressive futures, preterites and so on, simply by using the appropriate tense of **estar**.

2. Irregular present participles
The only part of this tense that can be irregular is the present participle:

- two common verbs (**dormir** and **morir**) change the **o** stem to **u**:

durmiendo sleeping
muriendo dying

some verbs change the **e** stem to **i**:

corrigiendo correcting (**corregir**)
sonriendo smiling (**sonreír**)
divirtiéndose enjoying oneself (**divertirse**)
me estoy vistiendo I am getting dressed (**vestirse**)

- and finally some verbs have a change in spelling from **i** to **y**:

leyendo reading (**leer**)
oyendo listening (**oír**)
destruyendo destroying (**destruir**)

NB: **ir** (to go) and **venir** (to come) are never used in progressives:

voy means I am going (this minute) and I go (in general)
vengo means I am coming (now) and I come (to town on Tuesdays),
and when the waiter shouts **¡ahora voy!** it means he's coming –
immediately!

You can also substitute **seguir** (to follow), **andar** (to walk) and **ir** (to
go) for **estar** in order to form other progressives. These verbs convey
the idea of keeping on doing a particular action:

sigue mirando he keeps on looking
anda buscando su carpeta he's looking around for his file

HANDY PHRASES

estoy buscando a mi hija	I'm looking for my daughter
¿qué estas comiendo?	what are you eating?
está bebiendo una copa en un bar cerca de aquí	he's having a drink in a bar near here

PRACTICE

1 To begin with an easy exercise: make these verbs progressive – but
  be warned, there's a trick or two! And by the way, what's the
  difference in meaning between the two versions?

  a) escribo una postal a Inglaterra
  b) leo una novela de Goytisolo
  c) vengo a tu casa ahora mismo
  d) voy a España de vacaciones
  e) telefoneo a mi esposo en Alemania

f) friego los platos después de la cena
g) arreglo la casa después del fin de semana.

2 Now for some difficult sentences in the present tense. Can you make them progressive? You could even vary things by using **venir**, **andar** or **seguir**, instead of the more usual **estar**.

a) Un equipo especial investiga las ramificaciones de la mafia en Barcelona.
b) El Ministerio de Agricultura estudia la posibilidad de enviar los camiones por transporte marítimo.
c) Se celebra en Buenos Aires una exposición oficial de productos españoles.
d) Hay muchos clientes que se quejan.
e) Llama por teléfono a su esposa.
f) Recorren todos los bares, cabarets y discotecas de la ciudad.
g) Hacemos lo que podemos.

Reflexive verbs

IN ENGLISH: Reflexive verbs are those for which the subject and the recipient of the action are the same. In a phrase like 'he hurts himself', the words 'he' and 'himself' refer to the same person. To hurt oneself is therefore a reflexive verb.

IN SPANISH: You use reflexive verbs in the same way as in English – but there are more of them and they are not always easy to recognize. In Spanish **levantarse** (to get up) is reflexive: as is **acostarse** (to go to bed). Many verbs come into this category of doing something to oneself (like putting on one's clothes, washing, shaving or getting ready in the morning). Once you see the underlying logic behind this sort of verb, you will easily remember that they are reflexive.

Other reflexive verbs like **enamorarse** (to fall in love) or **sentirse** (to feel) are not particularly obvious, and these have to be learned.

Still other verbs change their meaning according to whether they are reflexive or not – in other words, perfectly ordinary verbs can become reflexive and mean something different. For example:

casar to marry off   but **casarse** to get married
ir to go   but **irse** to go off, to go away
hacer to do   but **hacerse** to become
poner to put   but **ponerse** to become or to put on

1. Forming reflexive verbs

Use the ordinary form of the verb and put the reflexive pronoun in front of it:

me levanto	I get up	**nos levantamos**	we get up
te levantas	you get up	**os levantáis**	you get up
se levanta	he/she gets up	**se levanta**	he/she gets up
	you get up		you get up
		se levantan	they/you get up

This holds good for all tenses of the verb.

2. Irregular reflexive forms

In three cases the reflexive pronoun does not come in front of the verb:

• we've already seen how **-se** is added to the end of the infinitive. This is always true, whatever the pronoun:

voy a bañarme I'm going to take a swim
va a acostarse he's going to bed

• when telling people what to do (positive commands), the pronoun comes after the verb:

¡cállate! keep quiet!
¡pónte allí! stand there!

NB: When telling people what not to do (negative commands), the pronoun stays in the same place, in front of the verb:

¡no te pongas allí! don't stand there!

• thirdly, if using a reflexive present participle, the pronoun is added to the end of the verb:

sentándose, empezó a hablar sitting down, he began to speak

3. More uses for *se* in Spanish

Spanish uses the reflexive pronoun **se** a great deal in an impersonal way – that is, where English might use the words 'people', 'one', 'they' or 'you'.

se dice que el papa va a visitar they say the Pope is going to visit
   España Spain

se oye a Pablo	you can hear Pablo
se cree que habrá una explosión nuclear	it is believed there will be a nuclear explosion

HANDY PHRASES

se sale por aquí	you go out this way
se prohibe fumar	smoking forbidden
no se puede circular por esta calle	no entry
¿cómo se dice ... en español?	how do you say ... in Spanish?
no se preocupe usted	don't worry about it
aquí se habla español	Spanish spoken here
se cierra el lunes	closed on Mondays
se prohiben coches	cars prohibited
no se responde de los objetos perdidos	we are not responsible for lost property
me levanté a las ocho	I got up at eight
me acosté a las once	I went to bed at eleven
me puse el vestido azul	I wore my blue dress
me fui a bañar	I went off swimming
me voy al banco	I am going off to the bank

PRACTICE

1 Describe your morning routine using the following verbs. Remember you'll have to change **se** to **me**:

   a) levantarse a las siete
   b) ducharse a las siete y cuarto
   c) secarse a las siete y media
   d) vestirse a las ocho menos cuarto
   e) peinarse a las ocho
   f) ponerse el abrigo para salir a las ocho y cuarto

2 Now look at this passage about a truck driver. Underline all the reflexive verbs and give their infinitive forms.

   Yo viajo mucho. Soy camionero y representante. Me fui a Madrid a ver a unos amigos, dejé el coche en un garaje, me hospedé en un hotel ... bueno, pues, el domingo me puse a llamar a unos empleados pero no los pude localizar. Me puse muy nervioso, así que me vine inmediatamente de Madrid al pueblo.

3 Recipes are good examples of how to use the impersonal **se** – but the following one, for baked mushrooms, has been jumbled up. Can you sort out the correct order in which you would have to do the cooking?

a) se deja hervir cinco minutos
b) se lavan y se secan los champiñones
c) al final se pone todo en el gratinador para que se dore
d) se pone la mantequilla con la cebolla en la cazuela
e) se añade un poco de vino
f) se coloca todo en una fuente de ir al horno
g) se echan los champiñones y se revuelven bien
h) se les cortan y se pican

4 Finally here are some phrases about a third person. We want you to tell us about yourself – so put all the verbs in the first person, using **yo**. **NB:** one of them requires a spelling change.

a) se presentó en la casa de su novia, Elena.
b) se vestía muy bien con un traje azul marino.
c) se peinó antes de llamar a la puerta.
d) se acercó a la puerta principal.
e) se sentó a hablar con los padres.

The imperative

IN ENGLISH: We use imperatives (or commands) for giving instructions: 'cross now', 'open here', 'be quiet'. The verb doesn't change though – the forms cross, open, be, remain the same, no matter whom you're addressing.

IN SPANISH: Commands are used as in English, but there is a good deal of variation in the verb, depending on whether you are giving instructions to one or more people, and whether you address those people as **tú** or **usted**. Because of this variety, why not concentrate on learning the **ustedes** form? Or even easier, avoid the imperative altogether by using phrases like:

¿me hace el favor de (cerrar la ventana)?   would you mind (closing the window)?

¿quiere traer la cuenta?   would you bring the check?

WHEN TO USE

You will hear the imperative used a great deal in Spain, in stores, restaurants and on public transportation. Although English-speaking people would find the forms 'give me (a loaf of bread)' or 'bring me (the check)' somewhat abrupt, the Spanish find this way of speaking perfectly acceptable:

déme una barra de pan
tráigame la cuenta

You will also find the imperative used in signs and notices, though directions and instructions will sometimes use the infinitive instead. This is just a variation, but it's sometimes easier for the foreigner to assimilate.

1. Forming commands with *usted*

This is the form you will normally need on the street and in the stores.

● Take the first person present singular of the verb – if this ends in **o** – **traigo** (I bring)

● remove the **o** and add the opposite vowel – that is, **a** if you're dealing with an **-ir** or **-er** verb; **-e** if you've got an **-ar** verb:

traiga bring (**traer**)   **mire** look (**mirar**)

● If you are talking to more than one person, add a final **-n**:

traigan bring

● if you're telling people not to do a certain thing, use **no** in front of the verb:

no traigan don't bring

a) Some spelling irregularities

You can skip this section if you're not going to be writing Spanish:

● With verbs ending in **-car** (**buscar**) substitute **que** for **ce**, e.g. **busque** look for
● With verbs ending in **-gar** (**jugar**) change **-g** to **-gu**, **juegue** play
● With verbs ending in **-zar** (**comenzar**) change the **-z** to **c**, **comience** begin

b) More about forming commands

● Pronouns like **-se**, **-me**, **-lo** etc. are attached to the end of the command – if it's positive **tráigamelo** bring it to me. And you'll need a written accent on the vowel that you normally stress:

no quería dármelo he didn't want to give it to me

● If the command is negative, those pronouns remain in their normal position:

no me lo traiga   don't bring it to me

There are only two exceptions with polite commands – so we'll give them here:

vaya(n) a la tienda   go to the store
déme el diccionario   give me the dictionary

Once you've looked at the subjunctive mood, you will realize that these commands are the subjunctive forms for **usted** and **ustedes**. If you don't want to grapple with the subjunctive, however, learn the rules presented here and you won't have any problems forming commands.

2. Commands with *nosotros*
If you're with a group of friends, you might want to say 'let's …' (have a party, go to the beach, visit the Prado). You could use the imperative form (which would be the first person plural of the subjunctive, see p.48) but it's easier and more colloquial to use the phrase **vamos a …** :

vamos a dar una fiesta
vamos a la playa
vamos a ir al Prado

3. Forming commands with *tú* and *vosotros*
You will only need these forms if you are going to give orders to people whom you would normally address informally as **tú** – your family, friends and children.

a) positive commands with **tú**
Use this form when giving an instruction to a person you address as **tú**. It's simply the third person singular of any regular verb!

habla	he speaks	**¡habla despacio!**	speak slowly!
mira	he looks	**¡mira el mar!**	look at the sea!
escucha	he listens	**¡escucha la música!**	listen to the music!

b) irregular forms
There are eight common irregular commands with **tú**:

di	say	**sal**	go out
haz	do	**sé**	be
ve	go	**ten**	have
pon	put	**ven**	come

c) positive commands with **vosotros**

When you're instructing more than one person, take the infinitive form of the verb, remove the final -**r** and substitute -**d**:

(**hablar**) **¡hablad inglés!**   speak English!
(**poner**) **¡poned la mesa!**   lay the table!

If you're using a reflexive verb, then drop the intervening -**d**:

(**callarse**) **¡callaos!**   be quiet!

d) negative commands with **tú** and **vosotros**

Use the second person singular or plural of the present subjunctive with **no** in front of the verb. You'll find these forms on p.49.

¡no hagas eso!   don't do that!
¡no digas mentiras!   don't tell lies!

HANDY PHRASES

To attract the attention of the bartender or waiter, shout:

¡oiga!   listen! / over here!

When answering the phone, use **dígame** instead of *hello*.
When asking for an item in a store use:

déme (un kilo de peras)   give me (a kilo pf pears)
póngame (un kilo de uvas)   give me (a kilo of grapes)

In a restaurant when asking for the check use:

tráigame la cuenta   bring me the check

PRACTICE

1 a) You're in a café – you want to attract the waiter's attention. What would you say?
   b) Now you want the check. What do you say?
   c) You're in a **tienda de ultramarinos** – a grocery store. You want 200 grams of cheese. What do you say?
   d) Then you need two bottles of red wine. What do you say?
   e) You pick up the telephone when it rings. What is the first word you say?

2 You've asked for some directions in the street. Look at these replies and work out what they mean:

   a) vaya todo seguido
   b) siga por esta calle hasta el Corte Inglés

    c) doble a la izquierda
    d) no cruce por aquí – ¡está prohibido!
    e) salga del hotel y suba por la Gran Vía hasta la Plaza Mayor
    f) tome el autobús número diez y bájese delante del museo.

3 Finally, who would be likely to use the following commands?

¡Ponga en marcha la economía!   **a)** el primer ministro
                                              b) un fontanero
                                              c) un policía

Comiéncese por lavar y secar el pescado   **d)** un agente de seguros
                                              e) un cocinero
                                            f) un constructor

Echa el café en los recipientes y mételo
   en el congelador   **g)** una profesora
                                              h) una niñera
                                            i) una ama de casa

¡Haz tus deberes, niño!   **j)** una maestra
                                            k) un arquitecto
                                            l) un dentista

Tome estas pastillas cada cuatro horas   **m)** un médico
                                              n) una dependienta
                                              o) un abogado

The subjunctive mood

IN ENGLISH: The subjunctive is used very little – in fact, you may not be aware of it at all, except in phrases like 'if I were you' or 'be that as it may'. (The word 'may' is often an indication of the subjunctive.)

IN SPANISH: The subjunctive is used very frequently, not only in official language and in the newspapers, but in everyday conversation. However, if you think it will confuse you, skip this section and concentrate on recognizing subjunctive verb endings (see p.115). Sooner or later, though, in order to understand how Spanish works, you will find that you want to learn more about the subjunctive.

WHEN TO USE

The subjunctive is concerned with 'mood', with feelings, doubts and uncertainties. It is a mood of nuance and subtlety. This is why you won't need to use it when limiting yourself to very basic sentences such as:

quiero ir a España	I want to go to Spain
deseo comprar un vestido	I want to buy a dress

Generally the subjunctive is used, not as the main or principal verb but as a secondary one – a subordinate verb which somehow follows as a consequence of the first. Remember, subjunctive, subordinate:

quiero que tú vayas a España	I want you to go to Spain
deseo que ella compre un vestido	I want her to buy a dress

The subjunctive is usually used when the subject of the verb changes:

quiero ir a Madrid	I want to go to Madrid
quiero que mi esposo vaya a Madrid	I want my husband to go to Madrid

1. Forming the present subjunctive

● For **-ar** verbs take the first person singular of the present tense, remove the **-o** and add the following endings:

mirar	to look		
mir	e	mir	emos
mir	es	mir	éis
mir	e	mir	en

● **-er** and **-ir** verbs share the same endings:

escribir	to write		
escrib	a	escrib	amos
escrib	as	escrib	áis
escrib	a	escrib	an

NB: In the subjunctive, **-a** becomes **-e**, and **-e** becomes **-a**.

2. Forming the irregular subjunctive

If the verb is irregular in the first person of the present tense, then it will be irregular in the subjunctive:

salir: **salga**, **salgas** etc; **tener**: **tenga**; **tengas** etc; **venir**: **venga**, **vengas** etc.

With stem-changing verbs in **-ir** you make the usual changes from **e** to **i** and **o** to **u** – but there is an extra change in the first and second person plural:

pedir   to ask/to order   **pida**   **pidamos**
                                       pidas   **pidáis**
                                       pida   **pidan**

As one might expect, there are some subjunctives which are very irregular (**ir**, **ser**, **saber**, **dar**, **estar**, **haber** etc.). You'll find these forms in the verb list at the back of the book.

MORE ON WHEN TO USE

We've only included here three or four of the most common usages. Grammarians have written whole books on the Spanish subjunctive, so this section can only be a short summary.

● after 'wanting' verbs:

In the sentence 'I want my daughter to learn Spanish', we have two verbs ('want' and 'learn') and two subjects ('I' and 'my daughter'). The first verb (**querer**) is a verb of wanting: after verbs meaning to want, the second verb is always in the subjunctive:

quiero que mi hija aprenda español

● after verbs expressing orders:

pide al camarero que traiga una   she/he orders/asks the waiter for/
   botella de agua mineral   orders a bottle of mineral water

Note that here again we have two verbs and two subjects.

● after verbs suggesting doubt:

no estoy segura de que venga   I'm not sure he will come

● after verbs conveying emotion:

siento que te vayas . . .   I'm sorry you're going . . .

● after impersonal verbs:

es necesario que . . .   it's necessary that . . .
es mejor que . . .   it's better that . . .
es mejor que llegues temprano   it's better for you to arrive early

Finally, did you notice that the third person form is the same as the formal command? **Conteste** (answer), **venga** (come), **mire** (look) are really subjunctives: as are the informal negative commands **no mires** (don't look), **no pongas** (don't put), **no traigas** (don't bring).

The imperfect subjunctive

IN ENGLISH: This tense is usually translated by 'I might':

I might see you   he might come this evening

IN SPANISH: This tense is used under all the circumstances outlined for the present subjunctive – but when the first verb is in the past, use the imperfect subjunctive for the second verb:

quiero que venga	I want him to come
quería que viniera	I wanted him to come

The imperfect subjunctive, therefore, is a sort of past tense.

The imperfect is always used in conditional sentences – that is, sentences which follow the pattern: 'if ... , I would ...'

si fuera rico, no tendría que trabajar	if I were rich, I wouldn't have to work

1. Forming the imperfect subjunctive
There are alternative sets of endings for **-ar**, **-er** and **-ir** verbs. Start off with the third person plural of the preterite: remove the ending **-ron** and add either of the two endings below:

habl	ara	habl	áramos
habl	aras	habl	arais
habl	ara	habl	aran

habl	ase	habl	ásemos
habl	ases	habl	aseis
habl	ase	habl	asen

Both forms mean the same thing, so choose one and learn it well. If anything, the **-ra** form is more common and it might help you remember **quisiera** I would like – a phrase that's always cropping up.

Finally, the subjunctive is complicated – but that's what makes it interesting. Why not look out for it in signs, newspapers and in any information that comes your way? Once you're aware of its use, you will quickly become more accustomed to the subtleties of the Spanish language as a whole.

We're not going to ask you to practice the subjunctive, since that really goes beyond the scope of this book. Instead, study these examples and try to get a feeling for where the subjunctive is used:

con tanto calor, no hay quien trabaje
no quiero que te molestes lo más mínimo
¿sabes de algún instituto que quiera mantener correspondencia con chicas españolas?
el director no se quiere ir, pero los profesores quieren que se vaya
pidió que le diera una beca para estudiar en Londres
se pone la mantequilla en la cazuela, procurando que no tome color

Nouns

IN ENGLISH: Nouns can be masculine (John) or feminine (the waitress) but usually they are neuter – a house, the bag, the car.

IN SPANISH: All nouns are either masculine or feminine. In general, a word ending in **-o** is masculine: **el niño** (the boy) and a word ending in **-a** is feminine: **la niña** (the girl). Some other endings, like **-ción** (**la nación**, the nation) **-tad, -dad** (**la libertad**, freedom), **la ciudad** (the city) tend to be feminine also. These are only general guidelines though. It's a good idea to learn the gender of a word when you learn its meaning.

● There are of course exceptions to the **o**=masculine, **a**=feminine rule. Despite the **-o** ending, it's **la mano, la radio, la foto** and **la moto**.

● Some words have both genders and two meanings:

la cura is the (medical) cure and **el cura** is the priest
el orden is the order of a series, **la orden** the command
el guía is the tourist guide, **la guía** is the guide book or the telephone directory.

● Be careful with the singular form of the word **agua** (water). Although it's feminine, the Spanish say **el agua** – basically because it's difficult to say **la agua**. Treat it as a feminine word though:

el agua tibia   lukewarm water
las aguas medicinales   medicinal waters

1. Plurals of nouns

In English, we usually just add '-s' to a word to make it plural: one boy, two boys. To form the plurals of Spanish nouns simply add **-s** or **-es** to the singular form. If the word ends in a vowel (a, e, i, o, u) like **casa** (house), add **-s**: **casas** (houses). If the word ends in a consonant (the other letters), add **-es**: **señor**, **señores** **hotel**, **hoteles** **bar**, **bares**. If the word ends in a **-z**, change it to **-c-** and add **-es**: **lápiz**, **lápices** (pencil(s)) **nuez**, **nueces** (nut(s)).

2. Phrases with nouns

Here are some examples of how the Spanish use nouns.

In an advertisement for a restaurant, the locale is described as having:

calidad, imaginación y tradición (note all three nouns are feminine)

Here's what an antique shop had to sell in a recent auction:

dibujos, acuarelas y gouaches, libros, revistas, carteles, abanicos ...

Here's how a Spanish newspaper described an important personality:

abogado, periodista y filósofo, autor del libro *Vida en la Mancha*

and another:

nieto de José María Muñoz, tío de Pedro Saura, militar de carrera

PRACTICE

1 Here are the prizes to be won in a national contest in a woman's magazine. We think they could be more generous. Why not try doubling them? You'll have to know the word **dos** (two).

   a) una caja de turrón
   b) un jamón
   c) una bandeja
   d) un kilo de almendras tostadas
   e) un frasco de perfume
   f) una tableta de chocolate
   g) un delineador
   h) un tubo de crema antiarrugas
   i) un lápiz de labios

2 Now here's a list of the equipment you'll need for making a plant stand. We think it's going to be too big: can you make each item singular? You'll have to know **un/una** (one).

   a) 4 tablas de pino
   b) 20 clavos

    c) 15 tuercas
    d) 2 varillas de madera
    e) 2 asideras
    f) 2 planchas de aluminio

3 Finally, here's an advertisement for a vacation in Morocco. Like many advertisements, it's full of nouns and adjectives. Underline each noun in the plural – and give the singular form – and its gender.

Así es Marruecos. Un país de color y fantasía. En sus gentes, sus mercados, en sus palacios, en sus pueblos, en sus ciudades, en sus montañas, en sus playas ... descúbralo.

The definite article

IN ENGLISH: The definite article is the word 'the', used whether you're talking about things in the singular or in the plural.

IN SPANISH: There are four separate forms:

- **el** for one masculine noun   **el hombre**   the man
- **la** for one feminine noun   **la mujer**   the woman
- **los** for masculine plural nouns   **los hombres**   the men
- **las** for feminine plural nouns   **las mujeres**   the women

WHEN TO USE
Spanish uses the definite article more than in English. Look at the following examples:

el señor Suárez no está	Mr Suárez isn't in
los caballeros las prefieren rubias	gentlemen prefer blondes
me voy el lunes	I'm going away on Monday
la semana pasada	last week
el año que viene	next year

There are no hard and fast rules that determine when to use the definite article in Spanish – the best way is to get a feel for it from your reading and conversations with Spaniards.

1. Del/al

Spanish contracts the two words **de** ('of') and **el** ('the') to make **del** ('of the'):

el pasaporte del señor Smith　　　Mr. Smith's passport

The apostrophe **s** does not exist in Spanish, so you must always use the longer 'of the':

los folletos del guía　　　　　　the guide's pamphlets
los billetes del señor Melgar　　Mr. Melgar's tickets

A ('to') and **el** ('the') also contract to make **al** ('to the'):

¿vas al bar?　　　　　　　　　are you going to the bar?
vamos al café　　　　　　　　　let's go to the café

PRACTICE

1　Now look at this list of materials that are supposedly ideal for use with Supercola, a new brand of glue: **cuero**, **loza**, **cartón**, **madera**, **cristal**, **papel**.

　　Can you provide the definite article that goes with each one? You may have to look up the meanings in the dictionary.

2　And these are the stores which stock Supercola: **papelerías**, **droguerías**, **ferreterías** and **grandes almacenes**.

　　This time give the plural form of the definite article that goes with each sort of store. Is it the same in all cases?

3　Finally, here are two lists of phrases. Can you match them up to make sentences?

el consultorio	de Juanito
la oficina	de la tienda de ultramarinos
vamos	del doctor Fernández
volvemos	del mecánico, don Pablo
el taller	al garaje en la calle Preciados
la escuela	de la compañía de seguros

The indefinite article

IN ENGLISH: The indefinite article is either 'a' or 'an': a postcard, an envelope. (Think about why we use 'a' in one case and 'an' in the others.)

IN SPANISH: We use the word **un** for the masculine singular and **una** for the feminine singular:

un hombre y una mujer	a man and a woman

Unos and **unas** in the plural mean 'some':

unos hombres y unas mujeres	some men and women
unas pesetas y unos duros	some pesetas and some duros (five peseta pieces)

WHEN TO USE
In Spanish the indefinite article is not used as much as in English. Look at the following examples:

soy médico	I'm a doctor
soy cubana	I'm Cuban
mil pesetas	a thousand pesetas
otro hombre	another man
¡qué mujer!	what a woman!
no tengo libro	I haven't got a book
salió sin sombrero	he went out without a hat

Look out for more examples as you practice your Spanish.

1. The neuter article
There is another article in Spanish (**lo**), called neuter because it's neither feminine nor masculine. It is used to express general ideas or an undefined object:

eso quiere decir lo mismo	that means the same thing
lo peor fue ...	the worst thing was ...
lo que no me gusta es el pescado	what I don't like is fish

As you can see from these examples, **lo** is often used with adjectives (**importante, peor**) – see the next section.

PRACTICE
1 Give the indefinite article for each of the following words:

piso   cocina   comedor   salón   habitación   fincas
chalets   apartamentos   villas   casas.

2 Look at these sentences in Spanish and English. Can you match up
   the translations?

   1. y ahora viene lo gracioso ...
   2. sabía todo lo que hacía yo ...
   3. Carmen abrió la puerta lo justo para ver quien era.
   4. Lo que más me molesta es el ruido que hacen los vecinos.
   5. Si te gusta lo natural, debes ponerte perfumes cítricos.

   a) what most annoys me is the noise the neighbors make.
   b) if you like to be natural, then you should wear lemon perfumes.
   c) Carmen opened the door just enough to see who it was.
   d) and now for the funny part ...
   e) she knew everything I did ...

Adjectives

IN ENGLISH: Adjectives don't vary their form:

a green tree/some green trees

IN SPANISH: Adjectives must agree with the noun that they are
describing, in number (singular/plural) and in gender (masculine/
feminine). There are four rules to follow:

● If the masculine adjective ends in **-o**, then the feminine form ends
in **-a**. The masculine plural will be **-os** and the feminine plural **-as**:

un traje amarillo	a yellow suit
una falda blanca	a white skirt
unos pantalones negros	black trousers
unas gafas rojas	red glasses

● If the masculine adjective ends in **-e**, there is no separate feminine
form:

un sombrero verde	a green hat
una chaqueta elegante	an elegant jacket

and you add -s to form the plural:

sombreros verdes	green hats
faldas elegantes	elegant skirts

● If the masculine adjective ends in a consonant, there is no separate feminine form:

un traje gris	a gray suit
una falda azul	a blue skirt

add -es to make them both plural:

trajes grises   faldas azules

● Nationalities have four different forms:

el hombre francés	the French man
la señora española	the Spanish woman
los francos franceses	French francs
las pesetas españolas	Spanish pesetas

1. Position of adjectives

In English, the adjective is placed in front of the noun: a fascinating story, a marvellous man.

In Spanish, as you will have seen from the examples above, the adjective usually follows the noun:

un sitio encantador	a charming place
una mujer fascinante	a fascinating woman

But certain common adjectives often precede the noun – and when this noun is masculine, many lose their final -o:

un hombre bueno   a good man   but **un buen hombre**
un día malo   a bad day   but **un mal día**
el primer piso   the first floor
el tercer plato   the third dish/course
algún día   some day
ningún hombre   no man

Some adjectives change their meaning according to their position:

un hombre pobre   a poor man (not rich)
¡pobre hombre!   poor man!

NB: Grande is a special case: when it precedes a noun, it loses the **-de** ending, both in the masculine and feminine forms. It also changes its meaning to 'great'.

una gran señora   a great lady
un gran hombre   a great man
but **¡qué casa grande!**   what a big house!

HANDY PHRASES
You'll see these phrases on signs and notices in Spain:

agua potable   drinking water
días festivos   holidays
zona azul   blue zone (restricted parking)
estacionamiento limitado   (restricted parking)

and on menus, you might find the following items:

patatas fritas   French fries
pollo asado   roast chicken
salmón ahumado   smoked salmon
aceitunas negras   black olives

PRACTICE
1 Here's a short description of a woman. Underline all the adjectives and provide translations.

María, una mujer agradable, simpática y sencilla, según opinan todos los del pequeño pueblo andaluz en que vive: no tiene enemigos. Guapa, alta, elegante, conoció a Luis en una cafetería hace ocho años y se fue a vivir con él.

2 Here's a list of statements about people. Choose the adjective which you think is most appropriate.

a) María mide 1.78 – es muy: alta, fea, bonita
b) Juan pesa 90 kilos – es muy: flaco, elegante, gordo
c) José ya no tiene pelo – es: delgado, torpe, calvo
d) El bebé sólo tiene seis meses – es muy: pequeño, enfermizo, ruiseño
e) A Paco le gusta comer – es muy: comilón, borracho, atractivo.

3 And finally, here's an advertisement for a hotel in Madeira, with all the adjectives removed. Your job is to put them back – and make them agree with their noun:

Madera, una de las regiones más ...... de Europa. El hotel domina el océano ...... y la playa de arena ...... Bajo dirección ...... el hotel ofrece todas las comodidades ...... de Madera y de un hotel de esta clase. Ustedes descansarán en un ambiente ...... y ...... Hay dos piscinas ...... con agua ...... , todos los deportes ......, sauna, tenis y golf.

acuático tradicional sueco templado grande calentado
blanco elegante azul esofisticado

Comparative and superlative

IN ENGLISH: We compare one thing with another by using the phrase 'more ... than' or '...-er than':

this book is more interesting than the one I was reading yesterday
she's taller than her mother

IN SPANISH: We have the same phrase **más ... que**:

él es más listo que ella	he's brighter than she is
este jardín es más descuidado que el de al lado	this garden is messier than the one next door

If you want to use the superlative and say 'the most' (interesting, charming), then use the article as well:

es el más bonito de todos	it's the nicest one of all
son los más ruidosos del pueblo	they're the most noisy (noisiest) in town

Remember to make the adjective and the article agree with the noun. Some adjectives have special forms in the comparative:

mejor = better
este vino es mejor que ése	this wine is better than that one

peor = worse
esta habitación es peor que ésa	this room is worse than that one

mayor = older/est
mi hija mayor	my elder/oldest daughter

menor = younger/youngest
mi hijo menor	my younger/est son

NB: When talking about children, you will often hear **el más pequeño** because **menor** means under age **menor de edad**.

If you want to compare like with like, use **tan ... como**:

esta cerveza es tan buena como la otra	this beer is as good as the other
mi nuevo traje no es tan elegante como el otro	my new suit isn't as elegant as the other one

And if you're comparing amounts, use **tanto ... como**:

no me dieron tantas pesetas como ayer	they didn't give me as many pesetas as yesterday

Tanto is an adjective, so remember to make it agree with the noun.

HANDY PHRASES
You'll be using comparatives when you're comparing prices and sizes in stores:

¿tiene otro más grande?	have you got a bigger one?
¿hay otro más pequeño?	is there a smaller one?
¿hay algo más barato?	is there anything cheaper?

In a restaurant you might be asked:

¿quiere más patatas?	do you want more potatoes?
¿quiere más legumbres?	would you like more vegetables?

or you might want to ask for something less spicy:

algo menos picante por favor

1. Saying 'very' in Spanish
You may want to enthuse over something – a view, a meal, a party:

that was a very good meal
what a wonderful view!
that was a terrific party!

In Spanish, make an adjective superlative by using **muy** very:

era una comida muy rica	it was a very good meal

or by adding **-ísimo/-ísima** to the adjective:

era una comida riquísima	
es una mujer hermosísima	she's a very beautiful woman
es un político listísimo	he's a very clever politician

PRACTICE

1 First of all, a quick test. Can you make this sentence plural?

el coche del futuro – más rápido, más seguro, más barato.

And this one singular? Remember to change the verb to **es**:

son los más bonitos jerseys del invierno.

2 Now look at this passage and then answer the questions below:

Jeddah, la bellísima ciudad a orillas del mar Rojo por su tradición comercial, por su clima más suave, por ser etapa obligada de los peregrinos a Meca, es más relajada, más alegre, más viva que Ryad, capital artificial del reino.

a) Which is the only superlative in the passage?
b) What does it mean?
c) What does **más suave** mean?
d) How many other comparative adjectives can you find?
e) Can you make **suave** and **vivo** superlatives, using **-ísimo**?

3 Look at these sentences in Spanish and English. Can you match up the translations? By the way, **más ruido que nueces** is a proverb – which the Spanish are very fond of.

1. los más viejos del pueblo
2. el humor del dibujante es tan real como la vida
3. el mayor rendimiento con el mínimo gasto
4. un maquillaje de base más oscuro que el cutis
5. más ruido que nueces

a) much ado about nothing
b) make-up base that's darker than your skin
c) the cartoonist's humor is as real as life itself
d) the oldest men in the village
e) the best performance with the least expense

Demonstrative adjectives

IN ENGLISH: We use demonstrative adjectives when pointing to something or indicating one particular object in a group: this boy, that girl, those people.

IN SPANISH: Three different forms are used for this sort of adjective:

● **este** means 'this':

este hotel   this hotel
esta habitación   this room
estos vinos   these wines
estas botellas   these bottles

● **ese** means 'that':

ese bar   that bar
esa playa   that beach
esos clientes   those customers
esas españolas   those Spanish girls

● **Aquel** also means 'that' – but it's further away from you than **ese**:

aquel país   that country
aquella mujer   the woman over there
aquellos barcos   those boats in the distance
aquellas olas blancas   those white waves

NB: **este/ese/aquel** are adjectives: they must agree with the noun to which they refer.

If you intend to write in Spanish, you might be interested to learn that a written accent over **este**, **ese**, and **aquel** will turn the adjective into a pronoun:

nosotros estamos en este hotel, el Miramar	we're staying in this hotel, the Miramar
y nosotros en aquél, el don Juan	we're in the one over there, the don Juan.

WHEN TO USE

You'll probably find demonstrative adjectives most useful when you're out shopping. First study these two dialogues. The first one takes place at the shoe counter in a department store:

¿cuánto son estas sandalias?	how much are these sandals?
mil quinientas	1500 pesetas
¿y ésas?	and those?
lo mismo	the same
pues, me llevo este par	well, I'll take this pair then

Later on in a souvenir shop:

¿cuánto cuesta aquel jarrón?	how much is that vase?
novecientas cincuenta	950 pesetas
¿y esos azulejos?	and those tiles?
trescientas cada uno	300 pesetas each
bueno, déme este cenicero.	all right, I'll take this ashtray.
¿Cuánto vale?	How much is it?
¿éste? doscientas noventa	this one? two hundred and ninety pesetas

Demonstratives also crop up in introductions:

Pepe, ésta es Carmen	Pepe, this is Carmen
Carmen, éste es Pepe	Carmen, this is Pepe

PRACTICE

1 Can you replace the italicized word in each sentence with the word which appears in parentheses at the end? You will need to change the demonstrative adjectives so that they all agree.

a) Este *verano* será turbulento (primavera).

b) En esa *época* viajó a Méjico y a Estados Unidos (verano).

c) Sacaba fotos con aquellas enormes *cámaras* con trípode (cámara).

d) En aquellos *tiempos* vivía junto con su mujer (temporada).

e) Yo soy su esposa y no puedo hablar de estas *cosas* (tema).

Possessive adjectives

IN ENGLISH: The possessive adjective indicates who owns what: my car, your house, his camera.

IN SPANISH: They are used in the same way and translated as follows:

mi hija	my daughter	**mis hijos**	my sons/children
tu bolsa	your purse	**tus maletines**	your briefcases
su traje de baño	your/his/her/ their swimsuit	**sus gorros**	your/his/her/their bathing caps

nuestro hijo our son	**nuestros hijos** our sons/children
nuestra abuela our grandmother	**nuestras hermanas** our sisters
vuestro chico your boy	**vuestros sellos** your stamps
vuestra chica your daughter	**vuestras postales** your postcards
sus revistas your/his/her/their magazines	**sus periódicos** your/his/her/ their newspapers

WHEN TO USE

As you can see from the above table, **su** and **sus** are multipurpose – they mean 'his', 'hers', 'yours' or 'their'. This may seem confusing, but in practice you can tell what is meant from the context.

señorita, ¿es su toalla?	señorita, is this your towel?/Is this your towel, Miss?
Señor Altés ha dejado su pasaporte	Señor Altés has left his passport

● If you do want to make things absolutely clear, you could explain things further by adding **de**, the subject pronoun (see p.82). So, instead of:

tengo sus billetes I've got your tickets
you could say **tengo los billetes de usted**

instead of:
tengo su monedero I've got his wallet
you could say **tengo el monedero de él**.

However, don't use possessive adjectives when talking about clothes or parts of the body:

se me ha perdido el gorro	I've lost my bathing cap
me duele la cabeza	I've got a headache/my head hurts
los niños se pusieron el traje de baño	the children put on their swimsuits

NB: Traje de baño (swimsuit) is singular, because Spaniards assume each child has only one!

HANDY PHRASES

su carnet de conducir por favor	your driver's licence please
su pasaporte por favor	your passport please
su tarjeta de crédito por favor	your credit card please

If you're having trouble with your car you might want to say:

mi coche no arranca	my car won't start
he perdido las llaves de mi coche	I've lost my car keys

PRACTICE

1 Here's a list of the contents of your beach bag. Tell us they are yours by using the **mi** and then the **nuestro** forms:

bañador gafas oscuras bronceador gorro novela toalla sombrero crema chancletas.

2 Now look at the following passage. Underline all the possessive adjectives and think about what they mean. Then answer the questions below with **verdad** (true) or **mentira** (false).

Este año millones de españoles abandonarán sus casas en las ciudades y millones de extranjeros cruzarán nuestras fronteras. Pero muchos de los españoles que normalmente marchan fuera de España a pasar sus vacaciones se quedarán dentro de nuestro país – el valor de la peseta no da para mucho. Los viejos también se van de veraneo. Sus sitios preferidos son la playa, la montaña, o sus pueblos de origen. Prefieren ir con su familia y prefieren gastar su dinero en vacaciones que en acondicionar su vivienda o comprar electrodomésticos.

a) It's worth it for the Spanish to spend their vacations abroad this year.
b) Old people prefer to spend their money renovating their houses.
c) They prefer not to go on vacation with their families.
d) Many more Spanish people are staying in Spain this year.
e) Old people like visiting the places they come from.

3 Here's a list of the possible functions of a home computer. Change the possessives from **su** to **mi**. Remember to make them agree.

a) enseñar matemáticas a sus hijos
b) programar su dieta ideal
c) saber sus biorritmos
d) llevar su agenda profesional

4 Finally, study this extract from a woman's magazine. Note how the reader is referred to as **tú** or **vosotras** in order to achieve a chatty/colloquial style.

¿Os gusta nuestra portada con una modelo guapísima vestida de blanco? Podéis ganar el vestido en nuestro concurso – los detalles aparecerán en nuestro próximo número. Gracias también por todas vuestras cartas pidiendo labores. No caben todos aquí, así que veráis en las tiendas nuestra nueva revista – totalmente dedicada a labores. Estarán en las tiendas a partir del dieciocho de este mes.

Adverbs

IN ENGLISH: An adverb tells you more about a verb – how, when or where the action was performed. The adverb ending in English is often '-ly': slowly, badly.

IN SPANISH: The adverb is often formed from the feminine form of the adjective (if there is one) plus the ending **-mente**:

conduce rápidamente	he drives fast
camina lentamente	he walks slowly

but not always:

come demasiado	he eats too much
aquí se habla español	Spanish spoken here
anoche fuimos a una discoteca	yesterday we went to a disco

Some adverbs are formed by using **con** ('with') and a noun:

siempre conduce con calma	he always drives calmly
viene a España con frecuencia	he comes to Spain frequently

Look out for the adverbs **mal** and **bien**. They are often confused with the adjectives **malo** and **bueno**:

se come mal aquí	you eat badly here/the food is bad here

but,

la comida es francamente mala	frankly, the food is bad
habla bien el francés	he speaks French well

but,

habla un francés muy bueno	he speaks very good French

PRACTICE

1 Here's a list of adjectives. Can you make them into adverbs?

   reciente perfecto claro solo frecuente seguro tranquilo normal fácil personal oficial

2 Now here are some sentences. Give each one an adverb from the list you've just compiled. You may find that some adverbs will fit more than one sentence.

a) a mí me gusta hacer las cosas ......
b) visitó España ......
c) este viaje es el primero que ha hecho el rey de España ......
d) habló del tema ......
e) voy a pie ......
f) el jefe atiende a los clientes ......
g) habla el español ......
h) esto se hace ......

Numbers

IN SPANISH: Numbers are adjectives too – and some agree with the noun they describe. They can also vary for other reasons. You must know your numbers well if you are going to understand what things cost and when events take place.

1	uno	23	veinte y tres
2	dos	24	veinte y cuatro
3	tres	25	veinte y cinco
4	cuatro	26	veinte y seis
5	cinco	27	veinte y siete
6	seis	28	veinte y ocho
7	siete	29	veinte y nueve
8	ocho	30	treinta
9	nueve	40	cuarenta
10	diez	50	cincuenta
11	once	60	sesenta
12	doce	70	setenta
13	trece	80	ochenta
14	catorce	90	noventa
15	quince	100	ciento (cien)
16	diez y seis	101	ciento uno
17	diez y siete	200	doscientos (as)
18	diez y ocho	300	trescientos (as)
19	diez y nueve	400	cuatrocientos (as)
20	veinte	500	quinientos (as)
21	veinte y uno	600	seiscientos (as)
22	veinte y dos	700	setecientos (as)

800	**ochocientos (as)**	200,000	**doscientos (as) mil**
900	**novecientos (as)**	1,000,000	**un millon**
1000	**mil**	2,000,000	**dos millones**
2000	**dos mil**		

NB: The numbers 16–19 and 21–29 have two forms in Spanish. They can be written as either one or two words:

diez y siete or **diecisiete**
veinte y cuatro or **veinticuatro**

1. Points to remember
● First, if there's a one on the end of the number (**veintiuno**, **treinta y uno** etc.), drop the final **-o** of **uno** before a masculine noun:

veintiún duros but **veintiuna pesetas**
and
¿cuántos hombres vinieron? how many men came?
veintiuno twenty-one

● If you are talking about exactly one hundred things, use **cien** and not **ciento**:

cien pesetas but **ciento cincuenta dolares**

● The same applies before **mil**:

cien mil francos but **ciento cincuenta mil personas**

● Note the **-as** in parentheses after **doscientos**, **trescientos** etc., which means that these numbers must agree with the noun that follows. Since this noun is often **pesetas**, say:

doscientas pesetas, cuatrocientas pesetas

● Look out for **quinientos(as)** five hundred – the odd number in this section. It's important because there is a 500 peseta bank note in Spain that will often be given in change.

● **Mil** never changes – and it's always used in the first part of the date:

mil novecientos ochenta y cuatro 1984

● Finally, use **de** ('of') with the word **millón** million:

Inglaterra tiene cincuenta y dos England has fifty-two million
millones de habitantes inhabitants

2. Ordinal numbers
In English, we use ordinal numbers (1st, 2nd, 3rd) a great deal:

he was the tenth man in
it was our fifteenth wedding anniversary

In Spanish, you hardly ever hear ordinals beyond ten being used. After ten, use the cardinal numbers given above:

primero	1st	**sexto**	6th
segundo	2nd	**séptimo**	7th
tercero	3rd	**octavo**	8th
cuarto	4th	**noveno**	9th
quinto	5th	**décimo**	10th

You will probably come across ordinal numbers in your hotel or in a department store:

la primera planta the first floor (of a department store)
el tercer piso the third floor (of apartments)

PRACTICE

1 Recite out loud the following numbers in Spanish: 5, 10, 15, 20, 22, 31, 44, 58, 90, 99
 and for: 250 pesetas, 500 pesetas, 775 pesetas, 950 pesetas, 1000 pesetas.

2 Again, recite out loud the following dates: 1492, 1776, 1890, 1985.

3 Translate these phrases:

 a) my second son
 b) my first wife
 c) the first course
 d) the third floor

 You'll need to know the word **mi** my.

Time

IN ENGLISH: The two most important expressions we use are:

'what time is it?' and 'at what time?'

The reply to the first question will be something like 'it's ten after three' – and to the second 'at five after five'. Try to keep this clear in your mind when tackling the time in Spanish.

IN SPANISH: Instead of the word 'time', Spanish uses **hora** 'hour':

¿qué hora es?	what time is it?
es la una	it's one o'clock
son las dos	it's two o'clock
son las tres y veinte	it's twenty after three

● For the English 'past' or 'after' (e.g. twenty after four) use the word **y** 'and':

las cuatro y veinte	twenty after four
las dos y diez	ten after two

● And for the English 'to' (e.g. five to four) use **menos** 'minus':

las cuatro menos cinco	five to four
las ocho menos veinte	twenty to eight

● If you want to say:

in the morning	use	**de la mañana**
in the afternoon	use	**de la tarde**
in the evening	use	**de la noche**

for quarter and half, use the words **cuarto** and **media**:

son las cinco y cuarto	its a quarter after five
son las siete y media	its half past seven
son las once menos cuarto	its a quarter to eleven

son las ocho de la mañana
son las cuatro de la tarde
son las once de la noche

La tarde in Spain lasts longer than in English-speaking countries – usually until twilight.

● If you want to use 'in the morning', 'in the afternoon', 'in the evening' without specifying a time, use: **por la mañana**, **por la tarde**, **por la noche**:

por la mañana vamos al mercado, normalmente	we usually go to the market in the morning

NB: ¿A qué hora? at what time? English-speaking people often confuse this with the other time phrase **¿qué hora es?** **¿A qué hora?** means at what time (does the train leave, the bus arrive)? The answer will contain **a**:

a las dos	at two o'clock
a las once de la mañana	at eleven o'clock in the morning
a las cuatro en punto	at four o'clock on the dot

Remember in time expressions, if the question contains the preposition **a**, use **a** in the answer.

1. The twenty-four hour clock

In stations and airports you will see times posted according to the twenty-four hour system. The only extra word you will need to know is **cero** (zero):

14.05	**catorce cero cinco**
15.10	**quince diez**
20.35	**veinte treinta y cinco**

2. Making arrangements in Spain

You will need to know the days of the week and the months of the year when making travel arrangements or setting up appointments.

a) days of the week

lunes	Monday	**viernes**	Friday
martes	Tuesday	**sábado**	Saturday
miércoles	Wednesday	**domingo**	Sunday
jueves	Thursday		

- note that you don't use capital letters in Spanish.

- use the phrase **ocho días** (for a week) and **quince días** (for two weeks).

- if you want to say: I am coming on Monday   use **vengo el lunes**

- if you want to say: I come every Monday   use **vengo los lunes**

b) months of the year

enero	January	**julio**	July
febrero	February	**agosto**	August
marzo	March	**septiembre**	September
abril	April	**octubre**	October
mayo	May	**noviembre**	November
junio	June	**diciembre**	December

- again you don't need capitals with the names of the months.

- study the following date (taken from a letterhead):

Chicago, el seis de agosto de 1984

- note that you need to indicate the name of the place you're writing from

- you use cardinal numbers – apart from the first of the month: **el primero de octubre**

- you must use **de** before the year

- apart from the place name, no capital letters are used

c) dates

• don't use the English word 'on' in a sentence like:

we arrived in Spain on the third of August	**llegamos en España el tres de agosto**

• and if you want to ask what the date is, use:

¿qué fecha es? or **¿a cuántos estamos?**
The answer will be:
es el catorce de mayo ⎫
estamos a catorce de mayo ⎭ it's the fourteenth of May

HANDY PHRASES

It's well worth your while to learn some of these by heart: mark those you'll need to know and memorize them:

mediodía	noon
medianoche	midnight
a principios de (junio)	at the beginning of (June)
a mediados de noviembre	in the middle of (November)
a finales de (mayo)	at the end of (May)
¿qué día es hoy?	what day is it today?
es lunes	it's Monday
el sábado que viene	next Saturday
el lunes pasado	last Monday
la semana pasada	last week
hasta el viernes	until Friday
antes del sábado	before Saturday
después del domingo	after Sunday
ayer	yesterday
anteayer	the day before yesterday
mañana por la mañana	tomorrow morning
pasado mañana	the day after tomorrow

On your travels throughout Spain you might see the following signs – on a mailbox:

horas de recogida	collection times

on a shop door:

cerrado hasta el 1 de septiembre	closed until the first of September

on a church bulletin board:

horario de misas	times for masses

outside a castle, church or place of interest:

horario de visita	visiting hours

PRACTICE

1 Say the following times out loud: don't forget to use **son las ...**

a) 2.30 de la mañana   d) 8.20 de la tarde
b) 9.45 de la mañana   e) 10.40 de la noche
c) 5.55 de la mañana   f) 6.15 de la tarde

2 Now for some dates. How would the Spanish say?

a) the fourth of May
b) Monday, the 21st of June
c) Sunday, the 9th of February

3 Here's an extract (using the 24 hour clock) from the program guide to Spanish television's Channel 1. Answer the questions below in Spanish, using the 12 hour clock. Don't forget to use **a las ...**

14.00 Telediario
16.30 La tarde del lunes
17.00 El paraíso de los animales
18.00 Barrio Sésamo
18.30 La isla de coral
19.30 Un mundo feliz
20.20 Marco Polo
21.00 Telediario
21.35 De aquí para allá
22.05 Buenas noches

a) At what time is the first edition of **Telediario** shown? (the news)
b) And when is the second showing?
c) At what time are they showing **Barrio Sésamo**?
d) When does the programming begin?
e) And end?

Measurements

1. Distances
To ask how far one town is from another, use the following formula:

¿a cuántos kilómetros está Zaragoza de Barcelona?
how many kilometers is Zaragoza from Barcelona?

The reply will be:

Zaragoza está a 350 kilómetros de Barcelona
Zaragoza is 350 kilometers from Barcelona

or more simply:

está a 350 kilómetros
350 kilometers

HANDY PHRASES
¿está lejos?	is it far away?
si, está lejos	yes, it is
¿está cerca?	is it close?
si, está cerca	yes, it is
está a dos minutos	it's two minutes away

2. Quantities
Here it's a question of knowing that liquid is sold by the liter (**el litro**) or half-liter (**medio litro**).

Fruit, meat etc. is sold by **el kilo** or **medio kilo**.

Some items – like cheese, or cold cuts – are often sold by the gram.

HANDY PHRASES
un paquete	a package
una lata	a can
una bolsa	a bag
una botella	a bottle

● all these expressions will be followed by the preposition **de** of:

una botella de vino tinto	a bottle of red wine
un paquete de mantequilla	a package of butter
un kilo de manzanas	a kilo of apples
un litro de leche	a liter of milk
medio litro de aceite	half a liter of olive oil
una bolsa de patatas fritas	a bag of potato chips

doscientos gramos de queso manchego	200 grams of manchego cheese
una docena de huevos	a dozen eggs

3. Sizes
- When buying shoes, the important words to remember are:

número	size
usar	to wear

¿qué número usa (or calza)?	what size do you wear?
uso el 38	I wear size 38

- For clothes, the word to remember is **talla** size:

¿qué talla usa?	what size do you wear?
la 40 por favor	size 40 please

NB: With shoes use **el 38** (to agree with **número**) and with clothes **la 40** (to agree with **talla**).

PRACTICE
1 Here are two lists – one of measurements, the other of food items. Can you match them up?

una botella de	chocolate
un kilo de	mortadela
un paquete de	mantequilla
una lata de	vino blanco
doscientos gramos de	naranjas
un litro de	sardinas
una tableta de	leche

2 Now for some sentences about distances. Practice saying them out loud.

Madrid está a 50 kilómetros
Llafranch está a 200 kilómetros
Barcelona está a 500 kilómetros
Teruel está a 20 kilómetros
Zaragoza está a 220 kilómetros

(The numbers have been spelled out for you in the answers section.)

3 You're in a shoe store. The employee asks you what size you take.

a) Practice saying out loud: size 37; size 38; size 39.

b) And in a clothing store you are asked about dress sizes. Practice saying out loud: size 40; size 42; size 44.

What article will you use this time?

Questions

IN ENGLISH: There are four ways of asking questions, you can:

• change a statement into a question by reversing the order of the words:

I'm late   am I late?

• use phrases like wasn't it? aren't I? can't he?:

it was cold, wasn't it?
I am clever, aren't I?
he can do it, can't he?

• introduce questions with question words such as when? what? where? how?:

how are you?
when did you write that?
where are you going now?

• change the tone of your voice and turn a statement into a question:

you are going now
you are going now?

IN SPANISH: You can use the same four methods for asking questions. The most common one is the easiest: use exactly the same words as for a statement but change the tone of your voice so that it rises at the end of the sentence:

habla francés y alemán	he speaks French and German
¿habla francés y alemán?	does he speak French and German?
el hotel es muy caro	the hotel is very expensive
¿el hotel es muy caro?	is the hotel very expensive?

(You will notice that written Spanish has two question marks, one of which is upside down at the beginning of the sentence. The same occurs with exclamation marks. This simply warns you what sort of sentence is coming next.)

• You can also reverse the order of subject and verb as we do in English:

los chicos hacen mucho ruido	the children make a lot of noise
¿hacen mucho ruido los chicos?	do the children make a lot of noise?
usted es americano	you're American
¿es usted americano?	are you American?

• There are also question words such as **¿dónde? ¿cuánto?** etc.:

¿dónde está mi bañador?	where is my bathing suit?
¿a qué hora salimos?	what time are we leaving?
¿cuánto cuestan las entradas?	how much do the tickets cost?
¿cuántos nuevos vestidos te has comprado este verano?	how many new dresses have you bought this summer?
¿cuál es la mejor playa por aquí?	which is the best beach around here?
¿cómo es la nueva casa?	what's the new house like?
¿qué tal?	how are you? how are things?
¿de qué es esta camiseta?	what's this teeshirt made of?
¿quién es aquella muchacha?	who is that girl?
¿qué hay en el periódico?	what is there in the newspaper?
¿cómo se llama usted?	what are you called?

NB: There are accents on all these question words. But:

¿que hay por allí?	what is there around there?

and

ésta es la revista que compro normalmente	this is the magazine I buy normally

Cuánto/os (how many) must agree with its noun.

• Finally, the Spanish equivalent of isn't it?, won't you?, can you? is **¿verdad?** (really?) or **¿no?** (no?):

¿vienes con nosotros, verdad?	you are coming with us, aren't you?
¿te gusta España, no?	you do like Spain, don't you?
¿se marcha mañana, verdad?	you're leaving tomorrow, aren't you?
¿eres española, no?	you're Spanish, aren't you?

HANDY PHRASES

Here are a few of the more common questions you might ask or be asked in Spain (see also under 'question words' above).

a) in ordinary conversation:

¿dónde vives?	where do you live?
¿de dónde eres?	where are you from?
¿a dónde vas?	where are you going?

b) in a store:

¿qué quiere usted?	what would you like?
¿algo más?	anything else?
¿qué color quiere?	what color do you want?
¿qué talla quiere?	what size do you want?

c) in a bar:

¿qué hay de comer?	what is there to eat?
¿qué hay de beber?	what is there to drink?
¿cuánto es?	how much is it?
¿de qué es el helado?	what's the ice cream made of? (what flavor is it?)

d) among friends:

¿te gusta (España, Portugal, Galicia)?	do you like (Spain, Portugal, Galicia)?
¿no te gusta (el vino, la cerveza, la limonada)?	don't you like (wine, beer, lemonade)?

PRACTICE

1 Here are some questions and answers. Match each question with the most likely answers.

1 ¿dónde está el Banco de España?	**a)** de algodón fino
2 ¿Cuántas veces al año vienes a España?	**b)** el de limón
3 ¿A qué hora sale el tren para Barcelona?	**c)** que todavía no ha venido
4 ¿Cómo es tu novio?	**d)** en la Plaza Mayor
5 ¿De qué son estas camisas?	**e)** a las tres de la tarde
6 ¿Quién es aquella señorita?	**f)** dos veces por lo menos
7 ¿cuál quieres?	**g)** muy alto, muy guapo
8 ¿qué dices?	**h)** es una amiga mía

2 You're at the police station, reporting a stolen purse. How would you reply in English to the following questions? There are some past tenses in the questions, but you won't need them for your answers:

 a) ¿como se llama usted?
 b) ¿de dónde es?
 c) ¿cuál es su dirección en los Estados Unidos?
 d) ¿cuál es el número de su pasaporte?
 e) ¿en qué hotel está?
 f) ¿dónde estaba usted cuando le robaron el bolso?
 g) ¿qué hora era?
 h) ¿qué había en el bolso?

3 Here's a list of answers. Can you supply a likely question for each one?

 a) el talonario de cheques está en la mesa
 b) llegamos a las ocho en punto
 c) muy bien gracias
 d) ¿estos vaqueros? son de algodón
 e) ¿Paz? es una chica muy simpática

Negatives

IN ENGLISH: When we want to make a positive statement negative we use the words 'no' or 'not':

do you want to go to the movies? no, I don't.

IN SPANISH: The word **no** translates both English words 'no' and 'not':

¿quieres ir al cine? no, no quiero

Always put **no** in front of the verb – only object pronouns are allowed to come between them:

no veo a Carlos – no le veo en   I can't see Carlos – I can't see him
 ningún sitio   anywhere at all

IN ENGLISH: There are many other negative words – for example, 'nothing', 'nobody', 'never', 'none', 'neither'.

IN SPANISH: These words also exist but they must be positioned correctly within the sentence. Generally words like **nunca** (never), **nadie** (nobody), **nada** (nothing), follow the verb. If they do, they need an extra **no** before the verb:

no como nunca entre horas	I never eat between meals
no vendrá nadie aquí	nobody will come here
no tengo nada en el bolso	I haven't got anything in my bag

● If you want to emphasize the negative part of the sentence – you *never* drink wine, *nobody* ever comes to see you – put the negative word in front of the verb:

nunca bebo vino   nadie viene a verme

NB: In these cases, leave out the extra **no**:

no se olvida nunca de mandarles una postal	he never forgets to send them a postcard
nunca se olvida de mandarles una postal	

● **no ... ni ... ni** means neither ... nor/either ... or

no veo ni a Pedro ni a Luz	I can't see either Pedro or Luz

● **nada** and **nadie** can be used after prepositions like **con** and **sin**:

no se meta con nadie	don't get mixed up with anyone
se fue sin nada	he left without anything

● Don't be afraid to use lots of negatives in one sentence; Spanish is one language where two negatives don't make a positive:

no habla nunca con nadie	he never speaks to anyone

HANDY PHRASES

no gracias	no, thank you
nada más gracias	no more, thank you
no estoy de acuerdo	I don't agree
no sé	I don't know
no entiendo	I don't understand
no tengo hijos/pasaporte/coche	I don't have children/a passport/a car
no tengo nada que ver	I don't have anything to do with it
¡claro que no!	of course not!
de nada	you're welcome
no cuelgue	don't hang up (on the telephone)

PRACTICE

1 Answer these questions in the negative form.

   a) ¿vas mucho al cine?
   b) ¿entiendes el español?
   c) ¿viene mucha gente a la sala de fiestas?
   d) ¿tienes la grabadora y las cintas?
   e) ¿que tienes en el bolsillo?

2 Here we have two argumentative brothers. Whatever Eduardo says,
Roberto contradicts. Can you answer for Roberto?

Eduardo	He encontrado a mucha gente hoy.
Roberto	....
Eduardo	Siempre desayuno con café.
Roberto	....
Eduardo	Me recuerdo mucho del accidente.
Roberto	....
Eduardo	En Madrid tengo amigos y parientes.
Roberto	....

Subject pronouns

IN ENGLISH: These are the pronouns which replace the subject of the
sentence. For instance, instead of saying:
John takes the dog for a walk, you can say *he* takes the dog for a walk.
'I', 'you', 'he', 'it' – all these are subject pronouns.

IN SPANISH: The equivalents of these pronouns are:

yo	I	**nosotros**	we
tú	you	**vosotros**	you
él	he	**ellos**	they (masculine or masculine and
ella	she		feminine)
usted	you	**ellas**	they (feminine)
		ustedes	you

WHEN TO USE
These pronouns are not used nearly as much as in English because the
verb ending tells you who is performing the action. For instance, **hablo**

tells you who is speaking without adding **yo**. If you do say **yo hablo** instead of **hablo** you are stressing the fact that it's *you* doing the talking. **Tú** is used for those people you address informally – your children, your friends and your family. If you're talking to more than one friend, child or member of the family, use **vosotros**. **Tú**, however, is being used more and more frequently in conversation in the street and in stores – so if you don't want to appear standoffish, it's worth knowing. **Usted** and **ustedes** are used for people whom you address with more formality – people you don't know and people to whom you want to show respect. If you call someone Mr. Brown or Mrs. Smith in English, call them **usted** in Spanish. You often see **usted** and **ustedes** abbreviated to **Vd.** and **Vds.** or **Ud.** and **Uds.** Remember that you must use the third person form of the verb with **usted**: **usted mira** you look, **usted habla** you talk, **usted escucha** you listen.

PRACTICE

1 Would you address the following people as **tú** or **usted**?

a) your friend Charlie **b)** your neighbor's five-year-old daughter **c)** the bank teller **d)** a policeman **e)** your wife/husband **f)** Mr. Eric Smith.

2 Look at these phrases. Is the person being addressed as **tú** or **usted**?

a) ¿hablas español? **b)** ¿entiende el francés? **c)** ¿va muy a menudo a Mallorca? **d)** ¿dónde vives? **e)** ¿de dónde es?

NB: In Latin America, *ustedes* is used *both* for the formal and informal *you* (plural).

Direct and indirect object pronouns

DIRECT OBJECT PRONOUNS

IN ENGLISH: These are the pronouns which replace the object of the sentence. For instance, instead of saying:
Frank saw Tom in the conference room, you can say: Frank saw *him* in the conference room.
'Her', 'him', 'them' – these are all direct object pronouns.

IN SPANISH: It's possible to perform the same sort of substitution –

so as to avoid repetition and to make statements shorter and snappier.
The 1st and 2nd persons are easy enough:

me = me	**nos** = us
te = you (informal)	**os** = you (informal)

¡te veo Juanito!	I can see you Johnny!
os busco, niños	I'm looking for you children
no me entiende	he doesn't understand me
nos está mirando desde el balcón	he's looking at us from the balcony

1. Third person
This is a little trickier, because we are dealing with both things and people. Let's talk about things first.

a) *it* and *them*
If you're talking about one thing, use **lo** for a masculine word and **la** for a feminine word:

estoy buscando el periódico – no lo veo	I'm looking for the newspaper – I can't see it
estoy buscando la carta – no la veo	I'm looking for the letter – I can't see it

If you're talking about things in the plural, add **-s** to make **los** and **las**:

he planchado tus pantalones – aquí los tiene	I've ironed your pants – here they are (here you have them)
he planchado tus blusas – aquí las tiene	I've ironed your blouses – here they are (here you have them)

b) talking about people
Here again you must make the distinction between feminine and masculine, singular and plural. Talking about women, use **la** or **las**:

¿Mamá no está? no, la estoy buscando	isn't Mom there? no, I'm looking for her
¿las niñas no están? no, las estoy buscando	aren't the girls there? no, I'm looking for them

Talking about men, use **le** or **les**:

¿Papa no está? no, le estoy buscando	isn't Dad there? no, I'm looking for him
¿dónde están los chicos? no les veo	where are the boys? I don't see them

NB: La for a woman – **le** for a man.

INDIRECT OBJECT PRONOUNS

IN ENGLISH: In a sentence like

I gave the letter to John

'letter' is the direct object and 'John' is the indirect object. We can substitute 'to John' by 'to him'.

IN SPANISH: The equivalent of the above sentence would be:

di la carta a Juan	I gave the letter to John
le di la carta	I gave him the letter

Le is the indirect object. You'll be glad to know there is only one singular form **le** and one plural form **les**:

las chicas volvieron a casa y les di algo de comer	the girls came home and I gave them something to eat

Remember, **le** means to him/to her and **les** means to them.

1. Position of pronouns

In English, pronouns come after the verb:

Cathy saw me after school and gave it to me then

In Spanish, as you will have already seen, pronouns usually come in front of the verb:

Cathy me vio Cathy saw me

If there are two pronouns (gave it to me), put the indirect one first (**me lo dio**). And if both those pronouns begin with **l**, change the first one to **se**. This is done purely for sound – **le lo** is something of a tongue twister in Spanish:

se lo dije esta mañana I told him about it this morning

2. Some exceptions

As always, there are a couple of exceptions to the object-before-the-verb rule:

a) with positive commands, pronouns are added to the end of the verb:

   dímelo tell me about it

   but note:
   ¡no me digas! don't tell me!

b) and the same thing happens with a verb in the infinitive form:

   voy a dárselo ahora I'm going to give it to him now

   Did you notice the accents on **dárselo** and **dímelo**? This is to make sure that the word is stressed as it would be normally.

HANDY PHRASES

¿puede ayudarme?	can you help me?
¿puedo ayudarle?	can I help you?
¿puede darme (su tarjeta, su talonario de cheques)?	can you give me (your card, your check book)?
¿puede enseñarme (la catedral, la playa)?	can you show me (the cathedral, the beach)?
¿puede decirme donde queda (el banco)?	can you tell me where (the bank) is?
¿le molesto?	am I bothering you?
siento haberle molestado	I'm sorry to have bothered you
¿cuánto le debo?	how much do I owe you?

PRACTICE

1 First of all look at this table. See how many logical sentences you can make, using elements from each section e.g. **os enseño ahora** I'll show you now.

me		
nos	está mirando	
te	pagó	
os	interesa	ahora
lo	enseño	
la		mañana
le	escriben	ayer
les		

2 In the following sentences, the nouns have been replaced by pronouns. Can you put the nouns back in their correct positions? Remember that you'll have to do some reordering of the words.

a) Miguel la abre
b) ¿Les conoces?
c) Jorge se la quitó
d) Le vi en Santo Domingo el año pasado
e) La vi ayer en el Cine Rex

a Felipe y a Luis/al rey Juan Carlos/la camisa/la puerta/la nueva pelicula con Fernando Rey

3 The following phrases all contain pronouns. What do they mean?

a) ¿Puede darme la cuenta por separado?
b) Esto no es lo que quiero
c) ¿Puede recomendarnos un restaurante económico?

d) Te recojo en la calle Vicente Ferrer detrás del cine
e) Nos vemos mañana
f) Te ofrezco un helado
g) ¿Me baja el equipaje?

Possessive pronouns

IN ENGLISH: It is not always necessary – and indeed is rather long-winded – to repeat the full form of a noun and its possessive adjective. For instance, instead of saying:

there's my suitcase – where's your suitcase?
we might say:

there's my suitcase – where's yours?
Yours, mine, his, hers these are all examples of possessive pronouns.

IN SPANISH: It is also possible to avoid such repetition. The translation of the sentence we've just given you as an example would be:

allí está mi maleta ¿dónde está la suya?

La suya is the possessive pronoun which replaces **su maleta**. As you will have noticed **la suya** sounds (and is) singular and feminine – to agree with **maleta** suitcase. All possessive pronouns take the gender and number of the noun they replace. Here are all the forms:

el mío	la mía	los míos	las mías
el tuyo	la tuya	los tuyos	las tuyas
el suyo	la suya	los suyos	las suyas
el nuestro	la nuestra	los nuestros	las nuestras
el vuestro	la vuestra	los vuestros	las vuestras
el suyo	la suya	los suyos	las suyas

Here are some more examples:

mi madre y la tuya están fuera	my mother and yours are out
mi chaqueta está aquí pero ¿dónde está la suya?	my jacket is here – but where's yours?

This last example is ambiguous because **la suya** could mean hers, yours, theirs or his. Often the meaning will be perfectly clear from the context, but if it isn't then replace the pronoun with the longer **de él** (of him), **de ella** (of her), **de usted** (of you). Remember, though, not to use both forms in the same sentence! It's either **mi bolsa y la suya** or **mi bolsa y la de usted** my bag and yours.

And finally, you don't need to use the article (**el**, **la**, **los**, **las**) after the verb **ser** to be:

éste es mío   this is mine
¿es suyo?   is it yours?

PRACTICE

1 Study these sentences – especially the possessive pronouns. Then answer the questions in English.

   a) Juan, ¿has dejado las llaves en el coche? Y tú también, Marisa, has dejado las tuyas?

     What has Marisa left where?

   b) El mío vino la semana pasada para pasar unos días.

     The writer is talking about his mother/father/uncles/cousins.

   c) No encuentro mi maletín – y ¿dónde está el suyo?

     The writer is talking to his wife – or to an acquaintance?

   d) Nuestro hotel es muy bueno – de cinco estrellas y muy lujoso. El nuestro también es bueno, pero queda un poco lejos de la playa.

     What is a little far from the beach?

   e) ¿Vuestros suegros os van a acompañar de vacaciones? Los nuestros no, se quedan en Inglaterra para cuidar a los hijos.

     Who isn't going on vacation?

2 In the following sentences, the pronouns have been omitted and listed at the end of the exercise. Can you put them back?

   a) Conchita, este traje de baño es ......; ...... está en el coche.

   b) ¿Me prestas tu boli? Elena tiene ......

   c) Sus hijos están ya crecidos ...... todavía van a la escuela.

   d) La bicicleta es ......, el triciclo es ....

el mío	suyo	los nuestros
mía	el tuyo	mío

Relative pronouns

IN ENGLISH: Relative pronouns are used to connect two parts of the sentence together. They are words like 'that', 'who' and 'which':

that's the book which I want
that's the man whom I saw
that's the car that went past this morning

In English, the relative pronoun is often omitted:

that's the book I want
that's the man I saw

IN SPANISH: The most common relative pronoun is **que** meaning either 'who', 'that', 'which' or 'whom' – and it can be both singular and plural. Remember to use it! English-speaking people often mistakenly string phrases together without linking them with a relative pronoun:

la tienda que está en la calle del Mercado	the shop that's on Market Street
la guía que tienes no es muy buena	the guide book that you've got is not very good

● If you want to say 'whose' use **cuyo**. **Cuyo** is an adjective and must therefore agree with its noun – the word that follows it:

el gerente cuyo hotel está en la Avenida Miramar	the manager whose hotel is on Miramar Avenue
el chico cuyos padres están en la habitación al lado de la nuestra	the boy whose parents are in the room next to ours

● After a preposition (e.g. **de** of, **para** for, **con** with) use **quien** if you're talking about one person, **quienes** if you're referring to more than one:

¿de quién es esta tarjeta de crédito?	whose credit card is this?
¿con quienes vino?	which people/whom did you come with?

● If you're talking about things, use one of the forms of **el cual**: which form you use will depend on what you are referring to. For one masculine thing, use **el cual**, for one feminine thing **la cual**. **Los cuales** and **las cuales** are the plural forms. If the preposition is **de**, use **del cual**, **de la cual** etc.:

el banco delante del cual está Correos	the bank in front of which is the post office
la peluquería al lado de la cual hay una pastelería	the hairdresser next door to which is a bakery

In English, these forms sound rather stilted – as they do in Spanish! You won't hear them much or use them yourself but you will see them in newspapers and magazines. Written Spanish is a good deal more formal than the spoken language. On the other hand, you will hear **que** 'that' all the time – so please use it!

HANDY PHRASES

hay algo que no va bien en el coche/en el tostador/en la plancha	something's not working in the car/in the toaster/in the iron
¿crees que no viene?	do you think he's not coming?
Mallorca es más bonita de lo que pensaba	Mallorca is prettier than I imagined
¿tiene algo que le identifique?	do you have any identification?
quiero que me laven la cabeza y que me peinan	I want a wash and set

PRACTICE

1 Here are two jumbled lists of sentence parts. Match them up using relative pronouns.

es un ex jockey	a la vuelta
no me gustó la pelicula	recibe el premio
ésa es la señorita con	abandonó las carreras después de un accidente
es la primera vez	vimos ayer
el avión estaba más lleno a la ida	he hablado en el café esta mañana

Pronouns and prepositions

IN ENGLISH: After a short linking word, like 'for', 'to' or 'with' (that is, a preposition), we use ordinary direct object pronouns:

he used to go out with her
she gave the umbrella to him
what did she say to you?

IN SPANISH: We use the ordinary subject pronouns:

solía salir con ella	he used to go out with her
¿la merluza es para usted?	is the codfish for you?
no, para mi señora	no, for my wife
no, para él	no, for him

● There are, of course, some exceptions:
for me is **para mí**, for you (using **tú**) is **para tí**:

para mí, un café con leche – ¿y para tí, Olga?	coffee with cream for me – and what will you have, Olga?

These phrases often crop up when you're ordering in a café or restaurant, so learn them well.

NB: con 'with'. Here the whole word is lengthened: the first person becomes **conmigo** and the second **contigo**. The reflexive form is **consigo**:

¿vienes conmigo?	are you coming with me?
llévala contigo	take her with you

PRACTICE

1 How would you say in Spanish?
   for me   for her   to him   with me   with you (**tú**)
   to them   of hers

2 And now for some oral practice using **para**. Pretend you're in a café ordering drinks. Using **para mí**, **para tí**, **para usted** etc., order some items from the list below:

una coca-cola	una limonada
un café solo	una cerveza
un té con limón	una naranjada

Prepositions

IN ENGLISH: Prepositions are short, handy words like 'with', 'from', 'of', 'at', 'in', which show relationships of various kinds.

IN SPANISH: Translations for all these words exist but not every Spanish word always corresponds directly with its English equivalent. Let's look at each of the more important prepositions separately and see how they are used.

1. A
The most common Spanish preposition; it can be used to mean 'at', 'to', 'towards', 'on':

vamos a Madrid	we are going to Madrid
el banco está a la derecha, el hotel a la izquierda	the bank is on the right and the hotel on the left

Many English-speaking students of Spanish confuse **a** (and) **en** (in) – probably because of their memories of school French! Remember, **a** means 'to' or 'towards' and **en** means 'in':

vamos al bar	let's go to the bar
estamos en el bar	we're in the bar
vamos a España	we're going to Spain
estamos en España	we're in Spain

• use **a** with time expressions (see p.71):

¿a qué hora sale el avión?	at what time is the plane leaving?
estamos a veinte de mayo	it's the 20th of May
al día siguiente, fuimos todos a Marbella	the next day, we all went to Marbella

• use **al** (the combination of **a** and **el**) followed by the infinitive of a verb to mean 'on doing something':

al llegar al restaurante, pedimos una garrafa de vino tinto	on arriving at the restaurant, we ordered a carafe of red wine
al llegar a España, visitaremos todos los pueblos del sur	when we arrive in Spain, we will visit all the towns in the south

As you can see from these examples, **al** and the infinitive provides an easy alternative to the problem of tenses. In the first example, it's substituted for a past tense, in the second for a subjunctive.

• personal **a**:

This is what students of Spanish call the **a** that is placed in front of a person – if that person is the object of a sentence:

veo a Juan I see Juan but
veo la televisión I watch television

This **a** is untranslatable – but it must be used. You'll also need to use it with words like **nadie** (no one), **quien** (who), **alguien** (someone):

está visitando a alguien en Londres	he's visiting someone in London
no veo a nadie por aquí	I can't see anyone around here

HANDY PHRASES

a lo lejos	in the distance
a menudo	often
a pie	on foot
subir al autobus	to get on the bus
a 80 kilometros por hora	80 kilometers an hour
a tiempo	in time
a veces	sometimes
al lado de	next door to
a la derecha	on the right
a la izquierda	on the left

2. De

Use **de** where you would use 'of' in English:

es el coche de mi amigo	it's my friend's car
	it's the car of my friend

Remember the apostrophe s does not exist in Spanish: you must rephrase your sentence so that it reads – the car of my friend. English forms compound words very easily but Spanish doesn't. Phrases like bullring, bathing suit and living room are impossible in Spanish. You have to translate them with a phrase that includes **de** – **plaza de toros**, **traje de baño**, **sala de estar**.

• use **de** for saying where you come from:

soy de Chicago	I am from Chicago
soy de Edimburgo	I am from Edinburgh
soy de París	I am from Paris

- use **de** for 'about':

no sé nada de ella I don't know anything about her

- use **de** for what things are made of:

¿de qué es tu reloj? es de oro what's your watch made of? it's gold

- use **de** in time expressions:

a las seis de la mañana at six o'clock in the morning
muy de mañana very early in the morning
de día in the day
de ahora en adelante from now on

- use **de** to translate 'from' in phrases like:

una carta de una amiga a letter from a friend
una postal de mi primo a postcard from my cousin

HANDY PHRASES
de niño, era muy guapo as a boy, he was very good looking
la chica de ojos azules the girl with blue eyes
muero de hambre I'm dying of hunger
una máquina de coser a sewing machine
una taza de té a cup of tea
un vaso de vino a glass of wine
voy de Barcelona a Madrid I'm going from Barcelona to Madrid
el mejor hotel de la Costa del Sol the best hotel on the Costa del Sol

---

Por and *para*

IN ENGLISH: We have one preposition 'for', while Spanish has two: **por** and **para**.

IN SPANISH: Por and **para** are not interchangeable. Their uses are often rather subtle: time and experience will tell you when to use them. Here though are some general rules to help you get started.

1. Por

● use **por** for a specific period of time:

estoy aquí por tres semanas   I'm here for three weeks

● when you're exchanging one thing for another:

le doy cien pesetas por la mantilla   I'll give you a hundred pesetas for
the mantilla

● to mean 'for the sake' or 'because':

sólo vengo por los niños   I only come because of the
children

● to say 'by':

vinimos por avión   we came by plane

● in certain time expressions:

por la mañana   in the morning
por la tarde   in the afternoon
por la noche   in the evening

● for 'along' or 'through':

hay unas tiendas baratas por la   there are some inexpensive shops
calle de San Juan   on San Juan Street
tienes que pasar por Madrid   you've got to go through Madrid

● to mean 'per':

gano ocho dólares por hora   I earn eight dollars an hour

Because using **por** and **para** is a question of familiarity, here are some more examples using **por** for you to study. Can you see why it's used in each phrase?

HANDY PHRASES

tres por cuatro   three times three
entró por la puerta principal   he came through the main door
por lo que dicen, Granada es una   according to what people say,
maravilla   Granada is wonderful/
everyone says Granada is
wonderful
vamos a Madrid por Sevilla   we're going to Madrid via Seville

The most common phrases of all are **¿por qué?** (why?) and **porque** (because). You can tell the difference between the two in the following:

¿por qué llegas tan tarde?   why have you arrived so late?
porque perdí las llaves del coche   because I lost the car keys

2. Para

● use **para** to mean 'for' when referring to the person for whom something is meant:

una coca-cola para mí – ¿y para usted?	a Coca-Cola for me – and for you?

● for destination:

voy para Madrid	I'm leaving for Madrid

● in the words of the song:

voy para Cuba	I'm going to Cuba

(you can use **a** in this case too)

● if you can translate 'for' in English by 'in order to' (this will mean, of course, that you use it with a verb):

hemos venido para tomar el sol y para bañarnos	we've come to sunbathe and to go swimming

● use it in time expressions like:

tengo una cita para las tres	I've got an appointment at three
llegue para las dos	be there by two

HANDY PHRASES

un hotel para turistas	a tourist hotel
un regalo para tí	a present for you
no es para beber	it's not for drinking
tengo bastante para comprarte el traje	I've got enough to buy you the suit
estoy para salir	I'm about to go out

PRACTICE

1 The words **por** and **para** have been omitted in the following sentences. Can you insert whichever one you think is most suitable? Sometimes both **por** and **para** would make sense – but would mean different things.

    a) envíalo .... correo.
    b) lo obtuve .... un amigo.
    c) se cruza la frontera .... Canfranc.
    d) .... la mañana normalmente voy de compras en el mercado.
    e) vendí la tele .... seis mil pesetas.
    f) fuimos .... Madrid.
    g) tengo una carta .... tí.

h) no es .... comer.
i) salimos .... Cuba en 1936.
j) hazlo .... mañana.
k) son prácticas bolsas .... ir a la piscina o de compras.

Some final thoughts on prepositions

There are two important items to remember about prepositions. First, never finish a sentence with a preposition. We do this frequently in English with sentences like:

where do you come from?
there's the girl I was writing to
what's this made of?

In Spanish, the equivalents would be:

¿de dónde eres?
allí está la chica a quien escribía
¿de qué es esto?

Secondly, if a preposition is followed by a verb, the verb must be in the infinitive form, while in English you might find the present participle:

antes de escoger lo que vas a comer, ¡mira el menú!	before choosing what you'll have, look at the menu!
cruzó la calle sin mirar	he crossed the road without looking

Ser, estar, hacer

IN ENGLISH: We have only the one verb 'to be' – and that doesn't change very much! 'Is', 'are', 'was', 'were' – these are the most common forms of the verb.

IN SPANISH: There are two verbs for 'to be' – **ser** and **estar**. Besides having to grapple with tenses you will first have to decide which verb to use. Tomes have been written about the subtleties of these two Spanish verbs – so don't panic if you feel you're using the wrong one. You'll still be understood and with practice and more familiarity with Spanish speech you'll get a feel for when to use each verb. You'll find their forms on p.119 and 121.

1. Ser
● used for permanent characteristics – like a person's job, nationality or name:

soy enfermera	I'm a nurse
soy italiana	I'm Italian
soy María	I'm Mary

● for indicating where someone is from; what an object is made of; for ownership (all followed by **de** 'of'):

Pablo es de Madrid	Pablo is from Madrid
es de madera	it's made of wood
es de mi mujer	it belongs to my wife

● for telling time:

es la una	it's one o'clock
son las dos y cuarto	it's a quarter after two

● some adjectives may not necessarily seem very permanent – nevertheless they take **ser**:

es muy joven	he's very young
son muy gordos	they're very fat
es muy rica	she's very rich

2. Estar
● used for temporary conditions:

¿cómo está el agua?	what's the water like?
está fría hoy	it's cold today

● for talking about your health:

¿cómo está usted?	how are you?
estoy bien, gracias	I'm fine, thank you

● for talking about where things are:

¿dónde está Burgos?	where is Burgos?
está en el norte de España	it's in the north of Spain

● for forming progressive tenses (see p.39):

estamos tomando el sol	we're sunbathing
no me molestes – estoy leyendo	don't bother me – I'm reading

● and with past participles when these are used as adjectives:

el banco está cerrado	the bank is closed
las tiendas están abiertas	the stores are open

3. Some points to think about

Study these two sentences – they show you the vital difference between **ser** and **estar**:

¡estás muy guapa hoy!	you look very nice today (but not always!)
es una mujer guapísima	she's a very beautiful woman (she always was and always will be)

Here are some more examples – try to work out why **ser** is used in one sentence and **estar** in the other:

es de Alemania	he's from Germany
está en Alemania	he's in Germany
es un niño alegre	he's a happy child
está muy contento con su regalo	he's very happy with his present
está enfermo	he's ill
es un enfermo	he's an invalid
están cansados del viaje	they're tired from the trip
es un viaje muy cansado	it's a very tiring trip
es un chico muy molesto	he's a very annoying child
estoy muy molesto contigo	I'm very annoyed with you

on the telephone

soy Pedro	this is Pedro speaking
¿está Pedro?	is Pedro there?

3. Hacer

This verb has two basic meanings – to do and to make:

está haciendo un vestido	she's making a dress
nunca hace nada	he never does anything

It is used in several very common phrases:

● to mean 'ago' in sentences like:

hace un año	a year ago
hace seis meses	six months ago

● to mean 'for' in a sentence like:

hace un mes que estoy aquí	I've been here for a month

You'll see from this example that the second verb is in the present tense – because you are still here. Here's another example:

hace un año que trabajo en la biblioteca	I've been working in the library for a year

- in weather expressions:

hace sol   it's sunny
hace calor   it's hot
hace viento   it's windy

- finally, the reflexive form **hacerse** means to become:

se hizo médico   he became a doctor
se hizo enfermera   she became a nurse

PRACTICE

1 Would you use **ser** or **estar** in the following sentences?

    a) … médico. (*1st person*)
    b) cuando … joven solía ir a Méjico de vacaciones.
    c) María … morena, guapa y muy simpática.
    d) … estudiando en su cuarto. (*imperfect*)
    e) … de España. (*3rd person*)
    f) ¿dónde … Correos?
    g) hoy … mucho mejor. (*3rd person*)
    h) … con gripe. (*1st person*)
    i) … de mármol.

2 Now try translating these sentences.

    a) no sé qué hacer
    b) ¿qué haces aquí?
    c) les hice venir
    d) ¿cuánto tiempo haces que vives aquí?
    e) desde hace tres años
    f) se hicieron muy amigos
    g) se hizo abogado

Answers

The present tense

1 vendo, vendes, vende, vendemos, vendéis, venden; miro, miras, mira, miramos, miráis, miran.

2 soy de Italia, vivo en Milán; soy de Francia, vivo en París; soy de Alemania, vivo en Hamburgo; soy de los Estados Unidos, vivo en Nueva York; soy de Escocia, vivo en Edimburgo; soy de Inglaterra, vivo en Londres.

3 es muy caro; aquí está su pasaporte, señor; dos cafés por favor.

4 La historia se sitúa en los años treinta. Se inicia cuando el joven John y el médico del pueblo oyen un grito. Alarmados, van al lugar. Al fondo de un acantilado, ven a un hombre herido. ¿Porqué no le preguntan a Evans? son sus palabras. A partir de ahí, los hechos se complican . . .

The future tense

1 Here are just some examples of the sorts of sentences you could make: voy a ir (iré) a España la semana que viene; voy a estar (estaré) allí dos semanas; voy a viajar (viajaré) por el sur; voy a comer (comeré) paella y calamares; voy a beber (beberé) sangría y vino tinto; voy a visitar (visitaré) la Alhambra y Granada; voy a bailar (bailaré) todas las noches; voy a nadar (nadaré) en el mediterráneo; voy a mirar (miraré) a las chicas guapas; voy a escuchar (escucharé) música popular.

2 grabarán – grabar – to record, saldrá – salir – to come out; anunciará – anunciar(se) – to anounce; querrá – querer – to want.

3 a) seré responsable ... b) deberé ... c) tendré que ... d) será ... (does not change) e) deberé ... .

The conditional tense

1 compraría; viajaría; bebería; comería; escribiría.

2 You would have circled **a)** if you were in favor of Spanish entry **b)** if you were against **c)** if you wished to abstain and **d)** if you did not choose to reply.

   In the second survey, you would have circled **a)** if you would allow police entry without feeling annoyed, **b)** if you would allow entry but would feel annoyed and **c)** if you would not allow entry without an official permit.

3 podrían; encontrarían; se solucionarían; habría; tendrían; correrían; provocaría.

The imperfect tense

1 estaba; vivía; solían; tenía; trabajaba; enviaba.

2 montaba a bicicleta; nadaba en la piscina; tomaba un café; hacía footing por el parque; cambiaba dinero en el banco; compraba un vestido en Galerías Preciados; veía escaparates.

3 me disculpaba; hacía; decía; estaba; quería comprarme; tenía; veía; veía.

The preterite tense

1 **a)** He/she was born in London and died in New York at the age of sixty-nine. **b)** He/she died in Panama at the age of seventy-eight.

c) He/she died suddenly at his/her home in Madrid. He/she was one hundred years old.

2 fui al banco para cambiar dólares americanos; visité España para broncearme al sol; volví a mi habitación para cambiarme de ropa; conocí a Juan el año pasado en Gerona; quise comprar una entrada pero no quedaban asientos.

3 me lavé; me cambié; salí; fui; reunirme; crucé; caminé; vi; vi; di.

4 empezamos; bajamos; hicimos; pintamos; barnizamos; construimos; volvimos.

The perfect tense

1 a) ha b) has c) ha d) hemos e) han.

2 a) comido b) tomado c) ido d) comprado e) leído.

3 ha elegido; ha preferido; ha sido; ha seguido; ha cambiado; han tenido; he intentado.

The pluperfect tense

1 había hecho; había sido; habíamos visto; habían dicho; habías querido.

2 a) se habían contado b) habían sido c) había estado en contacto.

The progressive tenses

1 a) estoy escribiendo **b)** estoy leyendo **c)** vengo **d)** voy **e)** estoy telefoneando **f)** estoy fregando **g)** estoy arreglando.

In cases **a) b) c)** the use of the progressive tense implies that you are writing/reading/telephoning right now. The use of the progressive tense in **f)** and **g)** implies that you habitually wash the dishes after supper/clean the house after the weekend.

2 a) está investigando/sigue investigando **b)** está estudiando/anda estudiando **c)** se está celebrando **d)** se están quejando **e)** está llamando **f)** están recorriendo **g)** estamos haciendo.

Reflexive verbs

1 a) me levanto **b)** me ducho **c)** me seco **d)** me visto **e)** me peino **f)** me pongo.

2 me fui – irse; me hospedé – hospedarse; me puse – ponerse; me puse – ponerse; me vine – venirse.

3 b) h) d) g) e) a) f) c).

4 a) me presenté **b)** me vestía **c)** me peiné **d)** me acerqué **e)** me senté.

The imperative

1 a) ¡oiga! **b)** tráigame la cuenta **c)** póngame doscientos gramos de queso **d)** déme dos botellas de vino tinto **e)** dígame.

2 **a)** go straight ahead **b)** continue along this street until you get to the Corte Inglés **c)** turn to the left **d)** don't cross here, it's illegal! **e)** leave the hotel and go up the Gran Vía until you get to the Plaza Mayor **f)** take the number 10 bus and get off in front of the museum.

3 **a)** el primer ministro (the prime minister) **e)** un cocinero (a cook) **i)** una ama de casa (a housewife) **j)** una maestra (a primary school teacher) **m)** un médico (a doctor).

Nouns

1 **a)** dos cajas de turrón **b)** dos jamones **c)** dos bandejas **d)** dos kilos de almendras tostadas **e)** dos frascos de perfume **f)** dos tabletas de chocolate **g)** dos delineadores **h)** dos tubos de crema antiarrugas **i)** dos lápices de labios.

2 **a)** una tabla de pino **b)** un clavo **c)** una tuerca **d)** una varilla **e)** una asidera **f)** una plancha.

3 gente (f); mercado (m); palacio (m); pueblo (m); ciudad (f); montaña (f); playa (f).

The definite article

1 el cuero; la loza; el cartón; la madera; el cristal; el papel.

2 las papelerías; las droguerías; las ferreterías; los grandes almacenes.

3 el consultorio del doctor Fernández; la oficina de la compañía de seguros; vamos al garaje en la calle Preciados; volvemos de la tienda de ultramarinos; el taller del mecánico don Pablo; la escuela de Juanito.

The indefinite article

1 un piso; una cocina; un comedor; un salón; una habitación; unas fincas; unos chalets; unos apartamentos; unas villas; unas casas.

2 1d; 2e; 3c; 4a; 5b.

Adjectives

1 agradable/agreeable   simpática/pleasant   sencilla/unaffected pequeño/small   andaluz/Andalucian   guapa/beautiful   alta/tall elegante/elegant.

2 a) alta **b)** gordo **c)** calvo **d)** pequeño **e)** comilón.

3 más templadas; el océano azul; arena blanca; dirección sueca; las comodidades tradicionales; ambiente elegante y esofisticado; piscinas grandes; agua calentada; los deportes acuáticos.

Comparative and superlative

1 los coches del futuro – más rapidos, más seguros, más baratos; es el más bonito jersey del invierno.

2 a) bellísima **b)** very beautiful **c)** gentler **d)** three, más relajada, más alegre, más viva **e)** suavísimo, vivísimo.

3 1d; 2c; 3e; 4b; 5a.

Demonstrative adjectives

1 a) esta primavera será turbulenta **b)** en ese verano **c)** aquella enorme cámara **d)** en aquella temporada **e)** de este tema.

Possessive adjectives

1 mi bañador, nuestro bañador; mis gafas oscuras, nuestras gafas oscuras; mi bronceador, nuestro bronceador; mi gorro, nuestro gorro; mi novela, nuestra novela; mi toalla, nuestra toalla; mi sombrero, nuestro sombrero; mi crema, nuestra crema; mis chancletas, nuestras chancletas.

2 The possessive adjectives are as follows: **sus casas** their houses/homes; **nuestras fronteras** our borders; **sus vacaciones** their vacation; **sus sitios preferidos** their favorite places; **sus pueblos de origen** their towns of origin; **su familia** their family; **su dinero** their money; **su vivienda** their home.

a) mentira **b)** mentira **c)** mentira **d)** verdad **e)** verdad

3 a) mis hijos **b)** mi dieta **c)** mis biorritmos **d)** mi agenda profesional.

Adverbs

1 recientemente/perfectamente/claramente/solamente/frecuentemen-te/seguramente/tranquilamente/normalmente/fácilmente/personal-mente/oficialmente.

2 a) a mí me gusta hacer las cosas tranquilamente **b)** visitó España recientemente **c)** este viaje es el primero que ha hecho el Rey de España oficialmente **d)** habló del tema francamente **e)** voy a pie normalmente **f)** el jefe atiende a los clientes personalmente **g)** habla el español perfectamente **h)** esto se hace fácilmente.

Numbers

1 cinco; diez; quince; veinte; veintidós; treinta y uno; cuarenta y cuatro; cincuenta y ocho; noventa; noventa y nueve; doscientas cincuenta pesetas; quinientas pesetas; setecientas setenta y cinco pesetas; novecientas cincuenta pesetas; mil pesetas.

2 mil cuatrocientos noventa y dos; mil setecientos setenta y seis; mil ochocientos noventa; mil novecientos ochenta y cinco.

3 a) mi segundo hijo **b)** mi primera esposa **c)** el primer plato **d)** el tercer piso or la tercera planta.

Time

1 a) son las dos y media de la mañana **b)** son las diez menos cuarto de la mañana **c)** son las seis menos cinco de la mañana **d)** son las ocho y veinte de la tarde **e)** son las once menos veinte de la noche **f)** son las seis y cuarto de la tarde.

2 a) el cuatro de mayo **b)** lunes, el veintiuno de junio **c)** domingo, el nueve de febrero.

3 a) a las dos **b)** a las nueve **c)** a las seis **d)** a las dos **e)** a las diez y cinco.

Measurements

1 una botella de leche; un kilo de naranjas; un paquete de mantequilla; una lata de sardinas; doscientos gramos de mortadela; un litro de vino blanco; una tableta de chocolate.

2 Madrid está a *cincuenta* kilómetros; Llafranch está a *doscientos* kilómetros; Barcelona está a *quinientos* kilómetros; Teruel está a *veinte* kilómetros; Zaragoza está a *doscientos veinte* kilómetros.

3 a) el treinta y siete; el treinta y ocho; el treinta y nueve **b)** la cuarenta; la cuarenta y dos; la cuarenta y cuatro.

Questions

1 1d; 2f; 3e; 4g; 5a; 6h; 7b; 8c.

2 a) give your name **b)** your place of origin **c)** give your address **d)** give your passport number **e)** give your hotel **f)** give a location like **en la Plaza de España** or **en un café g)** give a time like **a las dos** or **a las diez h)** list some items like **mis cheques de viaje**, **mi pasaporte**, **tres mil pesetas**.

3 a) dónde está el talonario de cheques? **b)** ¿a qué hora llegaron? **c)** ¿cómo está? or ¿qué tal? **d)** ¿de qué son estos vaqueros? **e)** ¿cómo es Paz?

Negatives

1 a) no voy nunca al cine **b)** no entiendo el español **c)** no viene nadie a la sala de fiestas **d)** no tengo ni la grabadora ni las cintas **e)** no tengo nada en el bolsillo.

2 no he encontrado a nadie hoy; nunca desayuno con café; no me recuerdo nada del accidente; en Madrid no tengo ni amigos ni parientes.

Subject pronouns

1 a) tú **b)** tú **c)** usted **d)** usted **e)** tú **f)** usted.

2 a) tú **b)** usted **c)** usted **d)** tú **e)** usted.

Direct and indirect object pronouns

1 There are lots of possibilities – here are some: me pagó ayer; nos está mirando ahora; os enseño mañana; les escriben ahora.

2 a) Miguel abre la puerta **b)** ¿conoces a Felipe y a Luis? **c)** Jorge se quitó la camisa **d)** vi al rey Juan Carlos en Santo Domingo el año pasado **e)** vi la nueva película con Fernando Rey ayer en el cine Rex.

3 a) can you give us separate checks? **b)** this isn't what I want **c)** can you recommend an inexpensive restaurant? **d)** I'll pick you up in Vicente Ferrer Street behind the movie theater **e)** We'll see each other tomorrow **f)** I'll treat you to an ice cream **g)** would you bring down my luggage?

Possessive pronouns

1 a) her keys, in the car **b)** his father **c)** to an acquaintance **d)** the hotel **e)** the speaker's in-laws.

2 a) Conchita, este traje de baño es *mío*; *el tuyo* está en el coche. **b)** Elena tiene *el mío*. **c)** *los nuestros* todavía van a la escuela **d)** la bicicleta es *mía*, el triciclo es *suyo*.

Relative pronouns

1 es un ex jockey que abandonó las carreras después de un accidente; no me gustó la película que vimos ayer; ésa es la señorita con quien hablaba en el café esta mañana; es la primera vez que recibe el premio; el avión estaba más lleno a la ida que a la vuelta.

Pronouns and prepositions

1 para mí; para ella; a él; conmigo; contigo; a ellos; de ella.

2 You can make up lots of different orders – here are but a few examples:

para mí una coca-cola – ¿para usted? y para tí, ¿una limonada? una naranjada para él y un té con limón para ella.

Por and *para*

1 a) envíalo *por* correo b) lo obtuve *por/para* un amigo c) se cruza la frontera *por* Canfranc d) *por* la mañana normalmente voy de compras en el mercado e) vendí la tele *por* seis mil pesetas f) fuimos *por/para* Madrid g) tengo una carta *para* tí h) no es *para* comer i) salimos *para* Cuba en 1936 j) hazlo *para* mañana k) son prácticas bolsas *para* ir a la piscina o de compras.

Ser, estar, hacer

1 a) soy **b)** era **c)** es **d)** estaba **e)** es **f)** está **g)** está **h)** estoy **i)** es.

2 a) I don't know what to do **b)** what are you doing here? **c)** I made them come **d)** how long have you been living here? **e)** for three years **f)** they became great friends **g)** he became a lawyer.

Verbs and verb tables

This final section is divided into four parts: first, regular verb tables where you will find all the forms of the three verb types: **-ar**, **-er** and **-ir**. Then comes a section on radical-changing verbs, followed by another on verbs which have special spelling changes. Finally, there is an alphabetical list of the more common irregular verbs and verbs which have special meanings or take certain prepositions. Radical-changing verbs which occur in this list have their changes marked in parentheses. We'll only indicate the irregularities in the verb – other forms will be as usual. Prefix verbs won't be included because they behave just like their 'parent': for example, **convenir** (to agree) behaves like **venir** (to come) and won't be listed separately. Remember that in Spanish **ll**, **ñ** and **ch** are letters in their own right and will be found immediately after **l**, **n** and **c** respectively.

Now for some abbreviations:

inf = infinitive
rc = radical-changing
pret = preterite
imp subj = imperfect subjunctive
pres = present tense
pret = preterite tense
pp = past participle
pr subj = present subjunctive
fut = future tense
inf. command = informal command
for. command = formal command

REGULAR VERBS

	-ar	-er	-ir
infinitive	hablar *to speak*	aprender *to learn*	vivir *to live*
present participle	hablando *speaking*	aprendiendo *learning*	viviendo *living*
past participle	hablado *spoken*	aprendido *learned*	vivido *lived*
present	*I speak, am speaking, do speak* hablo hablas habla hablamos habláis hablan	*I learn, am learning, do learn* aprendo aprendes aprende aprendemos aprendéis aprenden	*I live, am living, do live* vivo vives vive vivimos vivís viven
imperfect	*I was speaking, used to speak, spoke* hablaba hablabas hablaba hablábamos hablabais hablaban	*I was learning, used to learn, learned* aprendía aprendías aprendía aprendíamos aprendíais aprendían	*I was living, used to live, lived* vivía vivías vivía vivíamos vivíais vivían
preterite	*I spoke, did speak* hablé hablaste habló hablamos hablasteis hablaron	*I learned, did learn* aprendí aprendiste aprendió aprendimos aprendisteis aprendieron	*I lived, did live* viví vivisto vivió vivimos vivisteis vivieron
future	*I shall speak, I will speak* hablaré hablarás hablará hablaremos hablaréis hablarán	*I shall learn, I will learn* aprenderé aprenderás aprenderá aprenderemos aprenderéis aprenderán	*I shall live, I will live* viviré vivirás vivirá viviremos viviréis vivirán

	-ar	-er	-ir
conditional	*I would speak*	*I would learn*	*I would live*
	hablaría	aprendería	viviría
	hablarías	aprenderías	vivirías
	hablaría	aprendería	viviría
	hablaríamos	aprenderíamos	viviríamos
	hablaríais	aprenderíais	viviríais
	hablarían	aprenderían	vivirían
perfect	*I have spoken*	*I have learned*	*I have lived*
	he hablado	he aprendido	he vivido
	has hablado	has aprendido	has vivido
	ha hablado	ha aprendido	ha vivido
	hemos hablado	hemos aprendido	hemos vivido
	habéis hablado	habéis aprendido	habéis vivido
	han hablado	han aprendido	han vivido
pluperfect	*I had spoken*	*I had learned*	*I had lived*
	había hablado	había aprendido	había vivido
	habías hablado	habías aprendido	habías vivido
	había hablado	había aprendido	había vivido
	habíaimos hablado	habíamos aprendido	habíamos vivido
	habíais hablado	habíais aprendido	habíais vivido
	habían hablado	habían aprendido	habían vivido
familiar commands (positive)	*speak*	*learn*	*live*
	habla	aprende	vive
	hablad	aprended	vivid
familiar commands (negative)	*don't speak*	*don't learn*	*don't live*
	no hables	no aprendas	no vivas
	no habléis	no aprendáis	no viváis
formal commands	*speak*	*learn*	*live*
	hable	aprenda	viva
	hablen	aprendan	vivan
present subjunctive	*I (may) speak*	*I (may) learn*	*I (may) live*
	hable	aprenda	viva
	hables	aprendas	vivas
	hable	aprenda	viva
	hablemos	aprendamos	vivamos
	habléis	aprendáis	viváis
	hablen	aprendan	vivan

	-ar	-er	-ir
imperfect subjunctive (-ra form)	*I (might) speak* hablara hablaras hablara habláramos hablarais hablaran	*I (might) learn* aprendiera aprendieras aprendiera aprendiéramos aprendierais aprendieran	*I (might) live* viviera vivieras viviera viviéramos vivierais vivieran
imperfect subjunctive (-se form)	*I (might) speak* hablase hablases hablase hablásemos hablaseis hablasen	*I (might) learn* aprendiese aprendieses aprendiese aprendiésemos aprendieseis aprendiesen	*I (might) live* viviese vivieses viviese viviésemos vivieseis viviesen

RADICAL-CHANGING VERBS

1 -ar and -er verbs: **o>ue**

contar (ue) to count
present cuento, cuentas, cuenta: contamos. contáis, cuentan
present subjunctive cuente, cuentes, cuente: contemos, contéis, cuenten
formal commands cuente, cuenten

2 -ar and -er verbs: **e>ie**

perder (ie) to lose
present pierdo, pierdes, pierde: perdemos, perdéis, pierden
present subjunctive pierda, pierdas, pierda: perdamos, perdáis, pierdan
formal commands pierda, pierdan

3 -ir verbs: **e>i**

pedir (i, i) to ask for
NB: Where there are two changes, the first is for the present, the second for the preterite and present participle.
present participle pidiendo
present pido, pides, pide: pedimos, pedís, piden
preterite pedí, pediste, pidió: pedimos, pedisteis, pidieron
present subjunctive pida, pidas, pida: pidamos, pidáis, pidan
imperfect subjunctive pidiera (-se), pidieras, pidiera: pidiéramos, pidierais, pidieran
formal commands pida, pidan

4 **-ir** verbs: **o>ue, o>u**

dormir (ue, u)   to sleep
present participle   durmiendo
present   duermo, duermes, duerme: dormimos, dormís, duermen
present subjunctive   duerma, duermas, duerma: durmamos, durmáis, duerman
imperfect subjunctive   durmiera (-se), durmieras, durmiera: durmiéramos, durmierais, durmieran
formal commands   duerma, duerman

5 **-ir** verbs: **e>ie, e>i**

sentir (ie, i)   to feel sorry, to regret, to feel
present participle   sintiendo
present   siento, sientes, siente: sentimos, sentís, sienten
preterite   sentí, sentiste, sintió: sentimos, sentisteis, sintieron
present subjunctive   sienta, sientas, sienta: sintamos, sintáis, sientan
imperfect subjunctive   sintiera (-se), sintieras, sintiera: sintiéramos, sintierais, sintieran
formal commands   sienta, sientan

VERBS THAT CHANGE SPELLING

1 Verbs ending in **-gar**:

pagar   to pay for
preterite   pagué, pagaste, pagó: pagamos, pagasteis, pagaron
present subjunctive   pague, pagues, pague: paguemos, paguéis, paguen
formal commands   pague, paguen

Other verbs like **pagar** are **jugar** (to play) and **llegar** (to arrive).

2 Verbs ending in **-car**:

explicar   to explain
preterite   expliqué, explicaste, explicó: explicamos, explicasteis, explicaron
present subjunctive   explique, expliques, explique: expliquemos, expliquéis, expliquen
formal commands   explique, expliquen

Other verbs like **explicar** are **tocar** (to touch), **equivocarse** (to make a mistake), **sacar** (to take out), **secar** (to dry) and **marcar** (to dial).

3 Verbs ending in **-ger** or **-gir**:

coger   to take hold of (things)
present   cojo, coges, coge: cogemos, cogéis, cogen
present subjunctive   coja, cojas, coja: cojamos, cojáis, cojan
formal commands   coja, cojan

Other verbs like **coger** are **dirigirse** (to go towards), **escoger** (to choose) and **recoger** (to pick up).

4 Verbs ending in **-zar**:

cruzar   to cross
preterite   crucé, cruzaste, cruzó: cruzamos, cruzasteis, cruzaron
present subjunctive   cruce, cruces, cruce: crucemos, crucéis, crucen
formal commands   cruce, crucen

Other verbs like **cruzar** are **aterrizar** (to land), **comenzar** (to begin), **empezar** (to begin) and **organizar** (to organize).

5 **-er** and **-ir** verbs with stems ending in **a**, **e** and **o**:

leer   to read
present participle   leyendo
past participle   leído
preterite   leí, leíste, leyó: leímos, leísteis, leyeron
past subjunctive   leyera (-se), leyeras, leyera: leyéramos, leyerais, leyeran

Other verbs like **leer** are **caer** (to fall), **creer** (to believe), **oír** (to hear) and **traer** (to bring).

6 Verbs ending in **-cer** or **-cir** preceded by a vowel:

conocer   to know
present   conozco, conoces, conoce: conocemos, conocéis, conocen
present subjunctive   conozca, conozcas, conozca: conozcamos, conozcáis, conozcan
formal commands   conozca, conozcan

Other verbs like **conocer** are **aparecer** (to appear), **nacer** (to be born), **ofrecer** (to offer), **parecer** (to seem), **pertenecer** (to belong to) and **reconocer** (to recognize).

IRREGULAR VERBS, VERBS WITH SPECIAL MEANINGS, VERBS + PREPOSITIONS

abrir	to open **he abierto** (perfect)
acabar de	+ inf. to have just. Use this verb in the present tense: **acabo de llegar** I've just arrived or in the imperfect: **acababa de llegar** I had just arrived
acordarse de	to remember (rc: **ue**)
acostarse	to go to bed (rc: **ue**)
alegrarse de	to be happy to
andar	to walk **anduve** etc. (pret) **anduviera** etc. (imp subj)
aprender a	to learn how to
apretar	to tighten (rc: **ie**)
asistir a	to be present at
atender	to attend, pay attention, look after (rc: **ie**)
atravesar	to cross (rc: **ie**)
ayudar a	to help someone to
conducir	to drive **conduzco, conduces** etc. (pres), **conduje** etc. (pret), **conduzca** (for. command)
contar	to count (rc: **ue**)
costar	to cost (rc: **ue**)
cubrir	to cover **cubierto** (pp)
dar	to give **doy, das** etc. (pres), **di, diste, dio** etc. (pret), **dé, des, dé** etc. (pr subj)
decidirse a	to decide to
decir	to say **digo, dices, dice, decimos, decís, dicen** (pres), **dije, dijiste, dijo, dijimos, dijisteis, dijeron** (pret), **diré, dirás** etc. (fut), **he dicho** (perf), **di, decid** (inf. command)
despertarse	to wake up (rc: **ie**)
doler	to be painful (rc: **ue**) **me duele el pie** my foot hurts
dormir	to sleep (rc: **ue**)
dormirse	to fall asleep
empezar a	to begin to (rc: **ie**)
encantar	to like very much **me encanta** I like it very much
encender	to light, switch on (rc: **ie**)
encontrar	to find (rc: **ue**)
enseñar a	to teach
entender	to understand (rc: **ie**)
escribir	to write **escrito** (pp)
estar	to be **estoy, estás** etc. (pres), **estuve, estuviste** etc. (pret)

faltar	to be missing **falta Juan** John's missing
freír	to fry **frito** (pp) **huevos fritos** fried eggs
haber	to have (auxiliary) **he, has, ha, hemos, habéis, han** (pres), **hube** etc. (pret), **he, habed** (inf. command), **hay** there is/are, **había** there was/were
hacer	to do/make **hago, haces** etc. (pres), **hice, hiciste, hizo, hicimos, hicisteis, hicieron** (pret), **haré, harás** etc. (fut), **hecho** (pp), **haz, haced** (inf. command)
importar	to matter **no importa** it doesn't matter
interesar	to interest **no me interesa** I'm not interested
invitar a	to invite
ir	to go **voy, vas, va, vamos, vais, van** (pres), **fui, fuiste, fue, fuimos, fuisteis, fueron** (pret), **iba, ibas** etc. (imp), **vaya, vayas** etc. (pr subj), **ve, id** (inf. command), **he ido** etc. (perf)
irse	to go off, to go away
llover	to rain (rc: **ue**) **está lloviendo** it's raining
morir	to die (rc: **ue**) **muerto** (pp)
mostrar	to show (rc: **ue**)
mover	to move (rc: **ue**)
nevar	to snow (rc: **ie**) **está nevando** it's snowing
oler	to smell (rc: **ue**) **huelo, hueles** etc. (pres) **huele a cebolla** it smells of onions **huela, huelas, huela, olamos, oláis, huelan** (pr subj)
olvidarse de	to forget to
pensar	to think (rc: **ie**) **pensar en** to think about
perder	to lose (rc: **ie**)
persuadir a	to persuade
poder	to be able (rc: **ue**) **podré** etc. (fut), **pude** etc. (pret)
poner	to put **pongo, pones** etc. (pres), **pondré** etc. (fut), **puesto** (pp), **puse, pusiste** etc. (pret), **pon, poned** (inf. command)
ponerse	to put on **me pongo el abrigo** I put on my coat to become **se puso pálida** she got pale
preferir	to prefer (rc: **ie**)
probar	to try (rc: **ue**)
quedar	to stay, be left **no me queda dinero** I've no money left
querer	to want (rc: **ie**) **querré** etc. (fut), **quise** etc. (pret)
quitarse	to take off **se quitó los zapatos** he/she took off his/her shoes

romper	to break **roto** (pp)
saber	to know **sé, sabes** etc. (pres), **sabré** etc. (fut), **supe** etc. (pret), **sepa** etc. (pr subj)
saber a	to taste of
salir	to go out **salgo, sales** etc. (pres), **saldré** etc. (fut), **sal, salid** (inf. command)
sentarse	to sit down (rc: **ie**)
sentir	to feel (rc: **ie**) **lo siento** I am sorry
ser	to be **soy, eres, es, somos, sois, son** (pres), **sea, seas, sea** etc. (pr subj), **fui, fuiste, fue, fuimos, fuisteis, fueron** (pret), **era, eras, era, éramos, erais, eran** (imp), **sé, sed** (inf. command)
servir	to serve (rc: **ie**)
servirse	to help oneself **¡sírvase!** help yourself!
soler	to be accustomed to (rc: **ue**) **suelo venir a España todos los años** I usually come to Spain each year
sonar	to ring (rc: **ue**)
sonar a	to sound like
tener	to have (rc: **ie**) **tengo, tienes** etc. (pres), **tendré, tendrás** etc. (fut), **tuve, tuviste** etc. (pret), **ten, tened** (inf. command)
tener que	to have to
traer	to bring **traigo, traes** etc. (pres), **traje, trajiste** etc. (pret), **traído** (pp)
tratar de	to try to
tratarse de	to be about, to concern **la película se trata de la guerra civil** the film is about (concerns) the civil war
valer	to be worth **¿cuánto vale?** how much is it? **vale** OK **val, valed** (inf. command)
venir	to come (rc: **ie**) **vengo, vienes** etc. (pres), **vendré** (fut), **vine, viniste** etc. (pret), **ven, venid** (inf. command)
ver	to see **veo, ves, ve** etc. (pres), **veía, veías** etc. (imp), **visto** (pp)
volver	to go back (rc: **ue**), **vuelto** (pp)
volver a	to do something again

Index